Cat Tales
of the
Old West

Poems, Puns &
Perspectives

On Frontier Felines

PRESTON LEWIS

San Angelo, Texas

ISBN: 9798218416256
Second Edition

Book Number One: Frontier Feline Series

Cover design by: Preston Lewis
Edited by: Harriet Kocher Lewis

Cover Photo Courtesy of the Library of
Congress

Library of Congress Control Number: 2024907779
Printed in the United States of America

DEDICATION

With Thanks and Appreciation
to
Dave Cheavens
David McHam
Harry Marsh
Adrian Vaughan
Mike Stricklin
Ed Kelton
Oscar Hoffmeyer
and
Harriet Kocher
Whose Lessons During
My Years at Baylor University
Made This and Other
Writing Projects Possible

.

CONTENTS

ACKNOWLEDGMENTS

Lessons learned at Baylor University years ago provided the foundation upon which this book and my previous publications have been built. Thanks to Dave Cheavens, David McHam, Harry Marsh, Adrian Vaughan, Mike Stricklin, Ed Kelton and Oscar Hoffmeyer for their journalism instruction during my college career. My most fortuitous college experience was meeting a young coed from Pennsylvania, Miss Harriet Kocher. In addition to taking my name as my wife, she is today my first and best editor and serves as editorial director of our Bariso Press. Specific to this project I must also thank Mike Cox, Beverly Waak and Jefferson Glass. Archivists who have been especially helpful over the years are Dr. Tai Kreidler of the Southwest Collection at Texas Tech University and Suzanne Campbell and Shannon Sturm of the West Texas Collection at Angelo State University.

Chapter One

The Cat-astrophic West

Some folks are cat people, others are not. I must admit that I am not a cat person. I am, however, a history person with a special interest in 19th century American history set in the western United States. My fascination with Old West history has roots in my West Texas heritage and a vacation when I was ten years old to Lincoln, New Mexico, where I walked the same street that Billy the Kid trod and became legend. During my writing career as a novelist, I have written three westerns with Billy the Kid as a character, but William H. Bonney is highly documented and researched by dozens of historians, many of whom I have met over the years at Western Writers of America conventions and historical association meetings.

Billy the Kid is a popular research topic, and though I enjoy him and other historical figures for my fiction, I prefer more obscure topics for my personal historical research. Cats in the Old West certainly fit my preference. How, you ask, did a person not enamored of cats start researching frontier felines? Blame it on Mike Cox, who was editor of the *Journal of the Wild West History Association* at the time. During a field trip to Fort Laramie during the 2016 Western Writers of America meeting in Cheyenne, Wyoming, our tour guide Jefferson Glass mentioned that on the Oregon Trail cats became a valuable commodity. Immediately, Mike turned to me and assigned me to write an article on cats in the Old West.

Over the years I have learned never to turn down an editor's request, especially when he's a friend of longstanding. So I began my foray into the history of frontier cats, beginning in my extensive library of western histories and biographies. Unfortunately, I found only limited references to cats in those books. In desperation, I turned to newspapers.com and entered "cats" in the search function. Immediately, a window into the past opened up for me on Old West cats. Doing a search for "cats" in all publications in the newspapers.com database between 1860 and 1900 identified 7,149,178 hits. For comparison, I searched for "dogs" and found 4,484,133 hits. Cats, it seemed, were on the minds of pioneers much more than dogs.

Though I came nowhere near viewing all 7.14 million cat references, I went through hundreds of them and found a broader picture of the colorful and often noisy history of frontier felines. No animal in the settlement of the Old West was more revered nor more reviled than the domestic cat, thanks largely to the law of supply and demand. Where cats were scarce, the demand for mousers was so great that dozens of entrepreneurs reaped exorbitant profits meeting the needs for pest control.

In towns where the cat population ran wild, residents demanded their feline companions shut up for a change so everyone could get a good night's sleep. In fact, the screeching, yowling and caterwauling of cats most certainly kept more folks awake at night in frontier communities than the gunfire of desperadoes or the whoops and hollers of cowboys celebrating on Main Street.

Not only did frontier cats make mews, but also news in papers that stretched the breadth of the westward migration from Missouri to California. If those papers are to be believed, cats were both the boon and bane of frontier existence and so newsworthy that editors plugged in stories not only about frontier cats but also their urbane though no more civilized counterparts back east. For *Cat Tales of the Old West*, I have culled dozens of the more entertaining or enlightening newspaper entries for publication. Most accounts had a local tie, but some were reprints of stories from eastern papers and even one from a London publication. Nineteenth century American newspapers often swapped editions with other papers statewide and regionally, granting each other permission to reprint stories in their own journals. This practice or "Exchange," as it was known, allowed papers to share news accounts, meaning that a cat story that first appeared in Texas might show up in Utah, muddying the actual location of the original incident. Often these clippings were marked as "Exchange" or "Ex." to designate their source. The criteria I used in selecting poems, stories and anecdotes for this collection was, first, that they had to appear in a newspaper west of the Mississippi

River and, second, that they were published before 1900.

Within those parameters, I began my research and came to some surprising findings. First, the nighttime noise of carousing and crooning cats remained a consistent problem with pussycats, especially during the year's warm months. Catcalls remained the persistent complaint of pioneers about their feline companions or, in many cases, antagonists.

Second, pioneers lacked modern sensitivities in dealing with the cat choruses, turning to bootjacks, guns, poison and other methods to rid the night of the noise.

Third, mining boomtowns set off cat rushes by enterprising entrepreneurs. From the California Gold Rush in 1849 to the Klondike strike starting in 1896, I found news accounts of clever individuals catching or buying cats and transporting them to the latest boomtown, where they sold them for ten to twenty times what they paid for them, turning a tidy profit for themselves and providing a public service to mining towns overrun with rodents.

Fourth, frontier cats endangered pioneers in ways missing in contemporary society. Rabid cats (as well as dogs) were common, consigning anyone who was bitten to a painful death. In an era when candles and coal-oil lamps provided much illumination in homes and businesses, cats remained a constant fire threat if they knocked over a candle or a lantern.

And fifth, felines despite their shortcomings remained an endless source of fascination for citizens of the Old West.

As a sample of my findings, I have compiled chapters on The Sound of Mews-ic; Nine Lives, More or Less; Mews-papers; Kiddy Letters; Cat-alists; Catsop's Fables and Tales; Purr-pose and Hiss-story; and Catcalls. I apologize for the puns, but cats just have a way of extracting them from the writers today and—as you will see—from the scribes of yesteryear. Some selections are written in dialect as they first appeared in print. Rather than try to make some spellings consistent—tomcat vs. tom-cat vs. Tom cat or pussycat vs. pussy cat vs. pussy-cat—I left them as originally printed in the 19th century. Some listed excerpts had headings, others did not. For readability and consistency, some headings have been added. Those headings have been italicized to differentiate them from original headings as they appeared in newspapers.

Most of what follows came from anonymous journalists and readers, whose names have been lost to history. However, to end this introduction, I chose to reprint a Bret Harte poem extracted from an 1874 Oregon paper. Though titled for the cat's perpetual antagonist, the verse reflects the humor and irony of a cat's life on the frontier. I hope you enjoy the poem and the subsequent *Cat Tales of the Old West*.

The Fate of a Fighting Dog
By Bret Harte

A man he owned a terrier dog—
  A bobtailed ornery cuss—
And that there purp got that there man
  In many an ugly muss;

For the man he was on his muscle,
  And the dog was on his bite,
So to kick the dog-gonned animile
  Was sure to raise a fight.

A woman owned a Thomas cat,
  That fit at fifteen pound;
The other cats got up and slid
  When that there cat was 'round.
The man and his dog come along one day
  Where the woman she did dwell,
And the purp he growled ferociously
  Then went for the cat like—everything.

He tried to chaw the neck of the cat,
  But the cat he wouldn't be chawed,
So he lit on the neck of that there dog,
  And bit! and clawed! and clawed!
Oh! the hair it flew! and the dog he yowled!
  As the claws went into his hide;
And the chunks of flesh was peeled from his back,
  Then he flummoxed and kicked and died.

The man he ripped, and cussed, and swore,
  As he gathered a big brick bat,
Then he would be darned essentially
  If he didn't kill that cat.
But the old woman allowed she'd be blest if he did,
  And snatched up an old shotgun,
Which was fired and peppered his diaphragm,
  With bird shot number one.

They toted him home on a window blind,
  And the doctor cured him up;

But he never was known to fight again,
  Or to own another purp.
Folks may turn up their snoots at this here rhyme,
  I don't care a cuss for that;
All I want to show is, that fighting dogs
  May tackle the wrong Tom cat.

> *Weekly Oregon Statesman*, Salem, Oregon
> Saturday, July 4, 1874, p1

Chapter Two

The Sound of Mews-ic

Far from the benign contemporary creatures that serve as pets or companions in many homes throughout the country today, cats on the frontier represented a nightly threat to the domestic tranquility as they roamed the streets, voicing their complaints against the world or seeking some companionship. Those roving felines meowed, purred, trilled, hissed, growled, snarled, grunted, screeched and wailed at all hours of the night.

The feline caterwauling came from perches as varied as fences, roofs, bushes, wagons, sheds, front porches and the neighbor's yard, invariably when folks were settling in for a good night's sleep. These nocturnal concerts drew the ire of sleepers and a variety of household items tossed through open windows at the carousing cats. If 19th century newspaper accounts are to be believed, the preferred ammunition of insomniacs was the common bootjack, an implement for holding a boot's heel to ease the removal from the foot. However, any object within reach would serve the same purpose, if only it flushed the mouser beyond hearing range.

Tossing objects at moonstruck mousers was so common that multiple news accounts tell of young boys going out late at night to impersonate cats, then collecting the objects tossed their way and hocking them the next day. This generally worked unless a frustrated sleeper fired some birdshot their way.

Keep in mind the dwellings of those times were far from airtight and outside noises permeated most homes, many having shutters rather than windows. On top of that, during the warm months, residents slept with open windows to draw a cooling breeze on hot nights. Such "open houses" not only allowed in drafts and insects but also the sound of mews-ic.

Silent Night Not

Often a stilly night,
  When stars their vigils keep,
And moonbeams, silvery bright,
  Through leafy branches creep—
A shrill, unearthly sound
  Comes through my window slats;
I rouse from sleep profound
  And mutter: "d—n them cats!"
    Las Vegas (N.M.) Free Press
    Tuesday, July 19, 1892, p3

Virtuoso

An exchange says that cats make good music—but it's after they have passed through the refining process and are properly adjusted and manipulated on the various string instruments.

> *The Red Cloud (Nebraska) Chief*
> Thursday, March 17, 1879

Moonlight Serenades

During these beautiful moonlight evenings cats' throats are having their spring openings.

> *Fort Scott (Kansas) Daily Monitor*
> Thursday, May 29, 1879, p2

Nightly Airs

When poets write
Of "voiceless nights,"
We feel like saying "rats!"
Because outdoors
We hear the roars
O' several hundred cats.

> *The Record-Union*, Sacramento, California
> Wednesday, January 1, 1890, p6

Soft Pitch

Leading musicians are advocating a lower musical pitch. We hope the cats will adopt it.

The Indian Advocate, Sacred Heart, Oklahoma
Saturday, Jan 1, 1898, p11

Punny Business

Somebody has discovered that the cat is not mentioned in the Bible. Yet there is the cat-e-chism.
— *St. Louis Post Dispatch*

The Weekly Chieftain, Vinita, Oklahoma
Friday, September 29, 1882, p3

Irresistible

Book-canvassers should take courage from a story told by an English lecturer on "The Art of Bookbinding."

A man of their profession had called at a house whose occupant met him with a growl.

"It's no use to me. I never read."

"But there's your family," said the canvasser.

"Haven't any family—nothing but a cat."

"Well, you may want something to throw at the cat."

The book was purchased.

The Medford (Oregon) Mail
Friday, November 23, 1894, p4

Man vs. Cat

A tom cat is a more independent animal than man.
When a man comes home at 2 or 3 o'clock in the
morning, he slips in as quietly as possible, but a tom
cat don't seem to care. The later the hour, and the
nearer the house it approaches, the louder it yells.
Jamestown (Dakota Territory) Weekly Alert
Thursday, August 15, 1878, p2

Sweet Music

The howling, barking, snarling and growling of some
seventy-five purps, accompanied by the melodious
strains emanating from two or three dozen tom-cats,
is about the sort of music which the ears of our
citizens have been regaled for several nights past. We
should not be surprised if a war of extermination
would be inaugurated before too long.
Feather River Bulletin, Quincy, California
Saturday, March 18, 1871, p3

The Thomas Cat

How doth the busy Thomas cat
  Improve each shining hour,
And test his vocal organs at
  The utmost of his power.

How neat he punctuates his yell,
  How well he rounds each claws,

While other tongues harmonious swell
  Feline do re me fas.

When others come within his reach,
  How neat he spreads the whacks;
While myriad voices yowl and screech
  In vocal cataracts.

Full oft his happy song is marred
  By wrathful man's attacks,
and morning shows the whole back yard
  Productive of bootjacks.
    Lawrence (Kansas) Daily Journal
    Sunday, November 16, 1873, p2

Will Be Pleased

Scientific minds will be pleased that the *New York Times'* scientist has discovered that electricity produces the nocturnal yowl of the honest house cat. "The cat perched on a back fence perpendicularly to the axis of the earth and to the direction of earth currents of electricity, howls because he—or she, as the case may be—is undergoing acute agony. Very possibly cats pass over fences running from north to south quite as frequently as they do over fences running in the direction of the equator, in the former case they experience no pain, and hence do not attract attention for their outcries. The moment, however, that a cat finds himself on an east and west fence he is racked by eternal pains; he tries to relieve his mind by howls and profanity, and he thereby excites the rage of his human audiences."

The Independent Record, Helena, Montana
Thursday, April 4, 1878, p1

Full of Fun

When a cat gives an entertainment from the top of a
wall, it isn't the cat we object to, it's the waul.
Abilene (Kansas) Daily Reflector
Wednesday, October 3, 1888, p4

Cat Story

Little pussy gave a squall,
Sitting on the garden wall;
Little pussy filled with pain
By a bootjack, squalled again
Little pussy met her Tom,
Commenced her discourse saying: "Dom,
Why have you been out so late?"
A brickbat struck her on her pate,
Then the lecture louder grew:
"O! meow, Tom! O! meow!"
Swelled her tail, raised her back,
Flew at her partner—that's a fact—
Just as naughty wives will do:
"O! meow, Tom! O! meow!"
When you won't supply the fam'
With cheese, or butter, lard or jam."
But, to resume, a chimney fell

Upon them both, and that was h—l.
'Twas just as good as a divorce—
One cat died, the other's hoarse.
>   *Las Vegas (N.M.) Free Press*
>   Thursday, January 28, 1892, p4

Too Much Cat

The *Lewiston Journal* says, there is a couple of spinsters in Green—monomaniacs in their way—who have been trying to see how many cats could be multiplied from one pair. They began with one pair when the rebellion broke out, and as the kittens have grown and multiplied their number now reaches the alarming sum of *four hundred and forty* cats and kittens.
>   *The Montana Post,* Virginia City, Montana
>   Saturday, October 8, 1864, p2

Poetry of the Period

A Thomas cat and an old bootjack
  Go hurtling through the yard,
The cat's ahead of the old rose-bed,
  But the bootjack's striving hard.

For the cat a fence of gleaming pine
  (Fences are handy for cats, I ween)!
A narrow post for him to climb
  (But the bootjack hit the mowing machine)!

Bootjacks and anthracite coal for you
  (Oh, the cat can scoot away)!

For me a corn and a misfit shoe
  (That hangs like a pall o'er a blighted day)!

For your profanity long and loud
  (Chaos where once order reigned)!
For I'm with bootjacks now endowed
  (Plant steel traps at my head)!
      Las Vegas (N.M.) Gazette
      Tuesday, August 30, 1881, p2

The Old Tom Cat

We have read a heap of gush about the voices of the
      night
When the moon is flooding Earthland with a sea of
      silver light,
When the stars are softly winking at each other in the
      skies,
And the breezes gently whisper atmospheric lullabies.
There are voices of the night that soothe a sleepy
      fellow's ear
Blended in a tender chorus that is mighty nice to hear,
But there always comes another one to knock their
      music flat—
That's the devilish soprano of the old Tom cat!

When the toil of day is over and the face begins to
      yawn
And the eyelids get to droopin' like their energy was
      gone,
Then we pull ourselves together, muster courage to
      unshuck.

And we think the bed the very softest snap we ever
    struck,
Pretty soon the vision-angel opens up his nightly
    show,
And we watch the fair dream pictures as they brightly
    come and go,
Till there comes a squally veto on such ecstasy as that
In the sleep-destroying solo of the old Tom cat.

In a voice he thinks is tender and a dream of harmony
He will perch upon the woodshed and will call his
    sweet Marie
And the two will get together and rehearse their tales
    of love
In a way t'd scare an angel from its roosting place
    above!
Then a fellow's Christian spirit always goes upon a
    strike,
And his words as wild as ever came resounding down
    the pike
As he hurls his household treasures out to interrupt
    the chat
Of that diabolic pussy and her old Tom cat!

We are weary of the story of the voices of the night
Told by dream-afflicted poets when they've nothing
    else to write,
For they pick the grains of sweetness from the chaff
    of painful fact,
And omit the sounds by which our ears are devilishly
    racked!
Why the dickens don't the scribblers fire a volley now
    and then

At the nuisance that makes demons of us meek and
    saintly men?
Cease to send their fancy pictures through the old
    poetic hat
And assault the nightly warbling of the old Tom cat?
— *Denver Post*
    Statesman Journal, Salem, Oregon
    Thursday, August 3, 1899, p3

The Festive Cat

The cat sings on the fence.
The cat is sad.
You can tell from the song it sings
Cats sing most when they are most sad.
The boy hears the cat and is sad too.
The boy has a toy gun.
He thinks if he could shoot it would make it less sad.
Kind boy!
At least it would make it sing less.
The boy hides behind the bush and shoots.
Has he shot the cat?
No, he has shot his pa.
How his pa howls!
He is the sad one now.
But the boy will be sad soon.
Will he be spanked?
You bet your uttermost picayune he will—spanked till
he is blue. — *Minneapolis Tribune*
    The Americus (Kansas) Ledger
    Friday, May 8, 1885, p3

A Back Yard Fight

They met on top of the backyard fence—an
    unconventional place—
And each one felt rather shy, upon seeing the other's
    face.
"I didn't know that the fence was yours;
Do you live in the big house there?"
But the little girl hugged her pussy cat,
And gave him a vacant stare.

"I've got a beautiful dog," said he, with a look full of
    scorning at
The bundle of gray that the small girl held—
Her beautiful pussycat.
And then the little girl found her tongue—
"Pussy can scratch and bite.
And if your dog is worth anything.
Why couldn't they have a fight?"

The little boy grinned from ear to ear; it wasn't the
    thing to do,
But maybe you would have grinned yourself,
If the little boy'd been you.
"He'll kill your cat, but if you don't care
It's be all right with me."
And he went to fetch the dog, with a heart
that was brimming o'er with glee.

Then at it they flew, with teeth and claws.
And the little boy cried, "It's fun."
Till he saw the cat was beating his dog.
Who'd nothing to do but run.
"Now, isn't he brave?" the little girl laughed.

As she kicked her heels on the fence.
And the little boy felt two inches tall
And dreadfully short of sense.

Then down he climbed, in his own backyard
And the world felt very flat.
And he wished instead of a frightened dog.
He had owned a pussy cat.
But such is the way of the world, alas,
And you'd best be sure you're right.
When you make a statement, but best of all,
Keep out of a backyard fight! — Mary Brent
Whiteside.

> *The Advocate*, Lakin, Kansas
> Thursday, March 16, 1899, p7

Bestseller

There is a new book entitled "How to Keep Dogs in
a City." A fortune awaits the author who will tell how
to keep cats out of a city.

> *The Advocate*, Lakin, Kansas
> Thursday, December 24, 1891, p3

Feline Diva

When a cat sings, does she do it on purr-puss?

> *Marysville (Kansas) Locomotive*
> Saturday, August 13, 1870, p1

Biblical Oversight

Someone has made the novel discovery that the cat is nowhere mentioned in the Bible. It is also observable that neither is the bootjack.

Black Hills (Dakota Territory) Daily Times
Thursday, May 24, 1883, p2

Pussycat Poetry

Cats are the poets of the lower animals; they alone cultivate the mews.

Lincoln County Tribune, North Platte, Nebraska
Saturday, June 2, 1888, p2

Singing Lessons

Father—That cat made an awful noise on the back fence last night.

Arnold—Yes, sir. I guess that since he ate the canary, he thinks he can sing.

The Record-Union, Sacramento, California
Friday, July 29, 1892

Spring Gleaning

Half a pound of shot administered to sympathetic cats at this season of the year will bear fruit in increased hours of slumber throughout the summer, and have a tendency to prevent a corner in the chicken market.

The Eureka (Kansas) Herald and Greenwood County Republican, Thursday, April 23, 1874, p3

No Stone Unturned

"Much remains unsung," as the tom cat remarked to the stone when it abruptly cut short his serenade.

Nebraska Advertiser, Brownville, Nebraska
Thursday, May 6, 1858, p1

Cat Houses

However well-behaved a family cat may be during the day; it cannot be trusted with a night-key after dark. There are too many lodges for cats at night. — *N.O. Picayune*

Dodge City (Kansas) Times
Saturday, May 8, 1880, p2

Peppermint Drops

A cat has nine lives, and it throws them all into its voice.

Omaha (Nebraska) Daily Bee
Sunday, December 29, 1889, p10

Painful Mockery

"I see in the paper," remarked a passenger from down East, "that a smart boy in Iowa made quite a strike by learning to imitate a cat. By going about in people's yards raising his caterwaul he made quite a spec of the old shoes, boot jacks, stove-handles and things he gathered up. But that is an old scheme. I tried the same thing when I was a boy and carried it on for two or three weeks. But one night, after making the air ring and shriek with my imitations, I concluded to give up the business. I was doing tolerably well for a boy, but all of a sudden I decided to quit, and quit I did.

"Couldn't you gather up enough stuff to suit you?"

"Enough" Should say I could. The very last thing I gathered in was a load of birdshot from a double-barreled shotgun. I always know when I've got enough."

Salt Lake Evening Democrat, Salt Lake City, Utah
Saturday, June 6, 1885, p3

Catnips

Ninety-four thousand two hundred and fifty-two cats in Kansas. A categorical statement. Let us hope they will get cataleptic fits. Scat.

Coffeyville (Kansas) Weekly Journal
Saturday, September 1, 1877, p1

Silent Night

Greenland has no cats. How thankful Greenlanders should be. Imagine cats in a country where the nights are six months long.

The Advocate, Lakin, Kansas
Thursday, April 13, 1893, p6

Dog Days, Cat Nights

Jones thinks that the saying "every dog has his day" is only the bark of a great truth, the body of which is that every cat has her night, and some nights a dozen cats. It is an unfeline conclusion.

Lawrence (Kansas) Daily Journal
Sunday, October 15, 1876, p4

Moonlight Serenade

"Does moonlight soothe?" asks the *New York Herald*. Well, no. It doesn't soothe the concert of cats that furnish the midnight mew-sic under our window. It takes old shoes, blacking brushes, ink bottles and everything else in the category to soothe them.

Arizona Daily Star, Tucson, Arizona
Wednesday, August 13, 1884, p2

A Catastrophe

"Did you see the account of the burning of the house of that old woman who lived alone with nine cats?"

"No, did the poor thing escape?"

"Yes, but the cats didn't."

"You don't say. The whole nine perished?"

"So the account says."

"That's a great loss to literature."

"How so?"

"Why the nine Mewses!"

Morning Oregonian, Portland, Oregon
Sunday, December 30, 1888, p11

Chapter Three

Nine Lives, More or Less

Death permeated the Old West, not just from the violence perpetuated in dime novels and later in movies, but also from diseases myriad and accidents innumerable. Because of death's many frontier permutations, pioneers lived a tenuous existence that inured them to the sensitivities of the modern mindset. When pioneers had seen friends and neighbors die or perhaps had dispatched another human being, the killing of a cat or dog appeared trivial in comparison. Too, if a westerner's sleep had been interrupted night after night by carousing cats, he was less likely to have any sympathy for the feline persuasion.

Old West newspaper accounts and commentaries reflected that insensitivity toward animals in general and cats in particular. Sometimes these observations came with humor, like the 1878 California paper reporting on a man who entered a gun shop. Asked if he wanted a six-shooter, the customer replied, "I'd rather have a nine-shooter. I want to kill a cat." An 1877 Kansas newspaper told of a "champion cat-destroying angel" that in 10 days killed "38 full-grown cats" by grabbing their tails and bashing them against a tree, a fence or a wall.

While curiosity may have killed the cat back east, out west the furry crooners were more likely to be shot, clubbed, lynched, buried alive or even fried. Reporting on a Virginia City, Nevada, fire that destroyed 2,000 buildings in a half-mile square of the business district, a Dallas newspaper noted, "There's a silver lining in the Virginia City cloud, in the fact that from 15 to 20,000 prowling pussycats are estimated to have gone up in the flames of the recent conflagration." Such was the life and death of cats in the Old West.

Why Nine Lives?

The sympathetic soul of Life says: "The cat has nine lives, which shows that nature had a pretty good idea what the cat would go through."
Paradise (Texas) Messenger
Saturday, June 21, 1890, p3

Loose Change

If I found half a dozen lead nickels in my change, I melted 'em up for bullets to shoot cats.
The Courier, Lincoln, Nebraska
Saturday, July 6, 1889, p7

More or Less Amusing

The latest popular song is entitled "The Tomcat Must not Yowl Tonight." It will be sent postpaid for $3, or with seven chambers and self-cocking action for $7.50 — *Burlington Free Press*
　　　Morning Oregonian, Portland, Oregon
　　　Thursday February 24, 1887, p4

Water Treatment

"Can you recommend anything for fleas on cats?" asks a correspondent. We can. Immerse the cat in four feet of water for two hours."
　　　Lincoln County Leader, White Oaks, New Mexico
　　　Saturday, December 3, 1887, p2

Feline Soloist

A tom-cat sits upon a shed
　And warbles wildly to his mate;
"Oh! when the world is gone to bed,
　I love to sit and mew till late."
But while this tom-cat sits and sings,
　Up springs a boarder, made with hate,
Who shoots that cat to fiddle–strings,
　He also loves to mutilate.
　　　Nebraska Advertiser, Brownville, Nebraska
　　　Thursday, November 18, 1880, p4

The Vanquished Cat

Out of the window a man
  Leaned with a look of despair,
Listening with haggard face to cat
  Whose melody rent the air.

But at last a ray of hope
  Lighted the man's despair.
Out of the window he leaned once more
  Into the damp night air.

A smile of infinite peace
  Over his features fell,
The song of the cat died out in the night
  As he rang his chestnut bell.
    Weekly (Salem) Oregon Statesman
    Friday, October 22, 1886, p2

Lines to a Cat

I love thee, cat; I love thy pleasant ways;
  I love to see thee dozing round the house;
I love, through all these dreamy summer days
  To watch thee circumvent the bashful mouse
I love to hear thy calm, contented purr,
And stroke thy coat—so near, and yet so fur.

But I love not, when starry night is come
  To hear thee, cat, with velvet-padded hoof,
Rapid as taps on the startled drum,
  Or summer raindrops, pattering on the roof.
For when thy claws slip, from their velvet jacket,

Thou art a wild Niagara cat—a cat a racket.

Sweet warbler, when the radiant moonlight falls
　In mellow splendor on the haunted shed,
Oft have I listened to thy plaintive wauls
　And cursed thee, from my sleep-deserted bed.
How have I wept to hear thy long-drawn shout,
"Maria! Oh-h Ma-ri-a! Comin' ou-out?"

Oh, cat ambitious! Thou wert born to lead;
　Thou are the first in peace, in war the furs;*
And to provide for each and every need,
　Thou never goest out without my purrs.
And like most human vocalists who sing,
You get back up, cat, at everything.

Why dost thou rage, vain cat, when sable night
　With "dewy freshness fills the silent air,"
Why dost though climb the roof to yell and fight,
　And rip and spit and snort and crawl and swear?
Dost though not blush, sweet cat, when rosy dawn
Sees half thy fur clawed out, and one eye gone?

Oh, cat, thou would'st not thus disturb the moon,
　If to the temperance pledge thou would's but stick;
Thou would'st not fight, unless at some saloon,
　Thou did'st get tighter, cat, than any brick.
I know you cat; I see it in your eye;
Full oft you take your catnips on the sly.

Go, gentle cat, go from my lap and prowl
　Upon the dizzy woodshed's beetling height,
On lofty dormer window sit and howl,
　And everything that weareth cat-hair flight.

And I will love thee still, for all of that,
Because I would not have the less a cat

Yet hear! When midnight pauses in the sky,
  I will arise from sleepless couch of mine,
And guided by thy animated cry,
  And by thine eyes so brilliantly that shine,
I will take down my trusty culverin,
And with six pounds of buckshot fill thy skin.
                    *It is also first on the woodshed
          Bismarck Tribune, Bismarck, Dakota Territory
          Saturday, August 2, 1879, p2

Man vs. Nature

Every dog may have his day and every cat his night;
every woman have her way, but man has nary a right.
For if he did he'd get his gun and shoot ten thousand
cats, he'd poison dogs just for the fun and fire theatre
hats. — Exchange
          Muskogee (Oklahoma) Phoenix
          Thursday, February 18, 1897, p4

Two Pussycats

        1. The Pet Cat
Dainty little ball of fur, sleek and round and fat,
Yawning through the lazy hours, someone's
        household cat,
Lying on a bed of down, decked in ribbons, gay;
What a pleasant life you lead, whether night or day.
Dining like an epicure, from a costly dish,

Served with what you like the best, chicken, meat or
    fish.
Purring at an outstretched hand, knowing but
    caresses;
Half the comforts of your life, pussy, no one guesses

Romping through the house at will, racing down the
    hall.
Full of pretty, playful pranks, loved and praised by all,
Wandering from room to room to find the choicest
    spot;
Favored little household puss, happy is your lot.

Sleeping on my lady's lap, or dozing by the grate,
Fed with catnip tea if ill, what a lucky fate!
Loved in life and mourned in death, and stuffed may
    be at that,
And kept up on the mantelshelf—dear pet cat.

2. The Tramp Cat
Poor little beggar cat, hollowed-eyed and gaunt,
Creeping down the alleyway, like a ghost of want,
Kicked and beat by thoughtless boys, bent on cruel
    play;
What a sorry life you lead, whether night or day.

Hunting after crusts and crumbs, gnawing meatless
    bones
Trembling at a human foot, fearing bricks and stones.
Shrinking at an outstretched hand, knowing only
    blows;
Wretched little beggar cat, born to suffer woes.

Stealing to an open door, craving food and heat.

Frightened off with angry cries, and broomed into the
    street;
Tortured, teased, and chased by dogs, through the
    lonely night:
Homeless little beggar cat, sorry is your plight.

Sleeping anywhere you can, in the rain and snow,
Waking in the cold, gray dawn, wondering where to
    go;
Dying in the street at last, starved to death at that;
Picked up by the scavenger—poor tramp cat. — Ella
Wheeler Wilcox
    The Democrat, McKinney, Texas
    Thursday, June 14, 1894, p4

Planting Time

An exchange says nothing can be more conducive to
the prosperity of a young grapevine than a cat planted
beneath its roots. It is not necessary that the cat
should be alive.
    Atchison (Kansas) Daily Champion
    Tuesday, June 6, 1871, p4

Goodbye, Pussycat

An Auburn man recently cured his cat of getting
upon the table in search of provender. He left some
nitroglycerine in a saucer close to the edge of the
table and poured a little milk on it, then went out and
waited. As he peeked through the window, he saw the
cat jump upon the table. He smiled.

Soon the cat found the milk, and in drinking it put its paw into the saucer. The man laughed aloud with glee. Then he heard a noise, and slowly got up from a cornfield over the fence, picked several cords of splinters out of himself and started into the house to see how the cat felt, but was surprised when he found the cat had gone and taken the house with her.
— Exchange

The Daily Tombstone, Tombstone, Arizona
Saturday, January 23, 1886, p2

Take Care

The *San Francisco Examiner*, unquestionably the wittiest sheet upon the coast, yesterday gave an example of its brilliancy. It dared to "get off" this: "Care will kill a cat. Therefore, when one goes hunting for cats, he should take care." We submit, that after this, the question should never again be raised that possibly some wittier journal than the *Examiner* may be evolved from the boundless future—the thing isn't possible.

The Record-Union, Sacramento, California
Thursday, October 22, 1885, p2

Feline Horticulture

Now is a good time to plant cats. The cats should be prepared with a club, revolver, or some other farming utensil, and then planted under a peach tree. If you have not got a peach tree, plant anywhere. Plant as many as you can, and plant deep. This branch of agriculture is much neglected — Greeley

Olathe (Kansas) Mirror
Thursday, August 29, 1872, p3

Rabid Advice

If your dog goes mad, kill your cat. That's good. We should never have thought of that remedy for hydrophobia, and what more appropriate than that the "feline" race should be made to suffer for the sins of the "canine." Your cure, Brother Cone, will work as a healing balm for future generations, and posterity will rise up and call you blessed.

The Osage County Chronicle, Burlingame, Kansas
Thursday, June 1, 1882, p1

Save the Ducklings

Rats, cats and weasels show a remarkable fondness for ducklings, and you have to look out for them. You can trap the weasels, circumvent the rats by housing the ducklings at night in rat-proof coops, and when you catch a stray cat making a dinner of young duck give her a lead pill to help on digestion; amputation of the tail just back of the ears will also cure pussy of this bad habit.

Council Grove (Kansas) Republican
Saturday, July 10, 1880, p1

Only Six Left

Papa Cat—Aren't you living rather fast, Thomas?

Young Thomas—Oh, no. I'm 1½ years old and have only lost three of my lives.

Papa Cat—Well, be careful, you young scamp! — *New York Journal*

The Advocate and News, Topeka, Kansas Wednesday, March 23, 1898, p15

Trapping the Cat

Our song and game birds have no deadlier foe than the common cat. The serpent destroys only when compelled by the pangs of hunger to seek his food. He fasts for more than half the year. The cat, cruel and cunning as the tiger, kills more than she can consume and, like the Berserkers of old, is mad with the love, of slaughter. Prowling by night through the forest and by stream, her path is dyed with blood. The young in the nest of the hare that escape her tiger fangs are fortunate.

As a household pet, she is a nuisance; as a destroyer of rats, a failure; as a companion, unsatisfactory and uninteresting, feeling but little affection for either friend or home; she is the sworn enemy of the farmer, killing the beautiful birds that are his friends and helpers; she is the unrelenting foe of the sportsman, and should be hunted down and destroyed like the wolf.

Almost any dog can soon be taught to chase and kill a cat; without this accomplishment he is but poorly educated. The breech-loader can only be used effectually by daylight, or when the moonbeams are very bright; but as the cat prowls most when the nights are dark in the lonely woods, where the ruffed grouse loves to lead her young, and through the stubble fields, where the quail have their playground, a deadfall placed here and there along the path is almost sure to arrest the midnight marauders. If a stream flows through the grounds, throw a tree across it and set your trap there. The cat dislikes to wet her feet, and will always use the bridge. As is well known, none of the feline race can resist the odor of valerian; to all of the tribe it is the elixir of life and the fountain of youth, and they will rush into any trap where it is. The skunk also loves it, and in his death agony will mingle his own perfume with it. If you set a deadfall and sprinkle under it some of the essential oil of valerian no Thomas or Tabitha passing near it will fail to enter and yield up the last one of the nine lives at the shrine of this great medicine god of the tribe.

The Record-Union, Sacramento, California
Saturday, March 26, 1881, p3

Gardening Tip

Cats buried in gardens afford the best sort of nourishment for growing shrubbery. The more cats buried the better.

Dallas (Texas) Daily Herald
Saturday, June 26, 1880, p4

The Dead Pussy Cat

You's as stiff an' as cold as a stone
    Little cat!
Dey's done frowed out an' left you alone,
    Little cat!
I'ze strokin' you' fur
But you don' never purr
Nor hump up anywhere,
    Little cat—
      W'y is dat?
Is you's purrin' an' humpin' up done?

An' w'y fer is you's little foot tied.
    Little cat?
Did dey pisen you's 'tummick inside,
    Little cat?
Did dey pound you wif bricks
Or wif big nasty sticks,
Or abuse you wif kicks,
    Little cat?
      Tell me dat,
Did dey holler w'enever you cwied?

Did it hurt werry bad w'en you died,
    Little cat?
Oh, w'y didn' you wun off and hide,
    Little cat?
I is wet in my eyes—
'Cause I almost always cwies
W'en a pussy cat dies,
    Little cat,
      T'ink of dat!
An' I'ze awfully solly besides!

Dest lay still dere in de sof' gwown,
    Little cat,
W'ile I tucks de gween gwass all awoun,
    Little cat.
Dey can't hurt you no more
W'en you's tired and so sore—
Dest sleep twiet, you pore
    Little cat,
    Wif a pat,
And forget all de kicks of de town. — Exchange
    The Butte (Montana) Miner
    Monday, March 5, 1894, p2

Chapter Four

Mews-papers

Because of their endless fascination among children, cats made regular appearances in the columns of Old West newspapers under regular headings such as "For Boys and Girls," "Some Good Stories for Our Junior Readers," "Our Young Folks," and "The Little Folks." The poems and stories offered laughs and lessons in life for the little ones.

Some stories amused and some informed children to the extent of the writer's knowledge at the time. The last entry refers to an old wives' tale that cats would suffocate infants by sucking the breath from their little lungs. Long before doctors identified Sudden Infant Death Syndrome or SIDS, grieving parents had few explanations for the death of their children under a year of age. While it is possible that cats on cold nights could have smothered babies by resting on their little heads for warmth, they never sucked the life from infants.

Instead, cats provided entertainment in ink that amused children and their parents when family entertainment options were limited after a hard day of chores on the farm, at the ranch or in town.

Letter from a Cat

Dear Editor: I hereby take
My pen in paw to say,
Can you explain a curious thing
I found the other day?
There is another little cat
Who sits behind a frame,
And looks so very much like me
You'd think we were the same.
I try to make her play with me,
Yet when I mew and call,
Though I see her mew in answer,
She makes no sound at all.
And to the dullest kitten
It's plain enough to see
That either I am mocking her,
Or she is mocking me.
It makes no difference what I play,
She seems to know the game;
For every time I look around
I see her do the same.
And yet no matter though I creep
On tiptoe lest she hear,
Or quickly dash behind the frame,
She's sure to disappear! — *St. Nicholas*
    The Advocate, Lakin, Kansas
    Thursday, June 1, 1899, p6

The Brave Little Mouse

Asleep in a chair lay Pussy-Cat-Mew,
  In his gray silk gown, so dainty and neat,
While out in the cold the March winds blew,
  And rattled the casements, and stormed and beat.

A bright-eyed mouse, in another gray gown,
  Had cuddled up close to Pussy-Cat-Mew
In the cushioned seat, and nestled down
  In a way no sensible mouse would do!

At last our Pussy-Cat-Mew awoke;
  He stretched himself in the easy chair,
And rubbed his eyes, and began to stroke
  His gray mustache—*and the mouse was there!*

"Aha, Miss Mouse!" growled Pussy-Cat Mew;
  (But brave Miss Mouse did not even wink.)
"This chair, as you see, will not hold two,
  And you are the one to go, I think!"

The mouse said neither "I won't!" nor "I will!"
  But only stared at Pussy-Cat Mew,
Who trembled with rage. "What! Silent still?
  To settle dispute I'll swallow you!"

Then the children cried, "Ho, ho! Ha, ha!"
  Till their laughter echoed through all the house."
"Come and see Pussy-Cat-Mew, mamma."
  Trying to swallow the rubber mouse!" — A.E.
Anderson
    The Record-Union, Sacramento, California
    Saturday, April 18, 1885, p6

Pussy's Complaint

I'm just as unhappy, unhappy,
  As ever a kitten can be.
If you'll let me, I'll tell you about it,
  And then perhaps you will pity me.
For it's a great mistake in you thinking
  That kits have no feelings at all,
Nor a thought beyond having a frolic,
  Or the chasing after a ball.
Now, how could I know (please tell me
  If you could help me to see)
That the cold roast fowl in the pantry
  Was not put there for me.
They left the door temptingly open,
  So I helped myself to that,
But they drove me out with the broomstick,
  And called me "that mean, thieving cat !"
Then those pans of milk in the dairy,
  With cream like the yellowest gold,
I thought I Should like to taste it,
  For it's very delicious, I'm told .
So I climbed to one of the nicest,
  And was just getting ready to taste,
When they found me—and such a commotion,
  I ran to the barn in hot haste.
Don't they think cats ever get hungry
  Between meals, I'd like to know?
And that rats and mice cannot always be found?
  I have sat for an hour or so
Beside some nice-looking rat-hole.
  And not even a mouse came to view;
And I found, after waiting and waiting,
  They had moved off to lodgings anew.

I heard the folks talking this morning
  About kit, and a bag, and the pond.
I didn't quite understand it,
  For of water I'm not very fond.
I don't dare to go near the kitchen,
  For fear they meant harm by that;
Oh, dear! all in all I've concluded,
  It's a very hard world— for a cat. — *Youth's Companion*
    The Record-Union, Sacramento, California
    Saturday, October 18, 1884, p7

The Wise Cat and the Foolish One

In the cozy kitchen the wise cat sat.
And she was glossy and sleek and fat.
Under the table she spied a can,
And swift to the shining vessel she ran,
Which some fish for the evening meal had held;
About its mouth she carefully smelled,
Then put in her paw and swept it round
Till many sweet morsels of food she found.
So you see by her wisdom the wise cat won
A nice little lunch, and no harm had been done.
That goes without saying; but how shall I tell
Of what a sad fate to the foolish one fell?
This cat to a deep hollow chancing to stray,
Where the can from the house had been thrown
      away,
Was starving for supper, and thought some to win
From the few flakes of fish that she saw within.
So she hurriedly thrust in her whole silly head;
But it proved a prison complete and dread,

And though here and there she frantically bounded,
The closer the terrible cap was pounded.
Exhausted at last, she was forced to lie
Quite still by the barn till a man happened by,
Who, pitying her, by dexterity
Succeeded in setting the poor creature free.
Now pussy, the wise, who had followed the man,
Seemed shyly to smile as this deed she did scan,
As much as to say, "What an ignorant cat!
I managed the matter much better than that."
But I think had she been hungry and cold,
She, too, might have grown as reckless and bold.
  The Record-Union, Sacramento, California
  Saturday, November 24, 1883, p2

The Three Kittens

In an old brick oven not far from here,
  All cuddled up in a heap.
Are three little kittens so cunningly dear;
Their story I know you will like to hear
  While they are fast asleep.

Two are spotted with white, one is soberly gray;
  Save the paws so soft and white,
Which with ashes and coals so frequently play,
And into all mischief so constantly stray.
  And oft are as black as night.

These are not the kittens of whom you have heard,
  Who lost their mittens one day,
For they are so wise they think it absurd

To put gloves on the claws of a kitten or bird,
  Who have only time to play.

Round and round they run, in the funniest style,
  After each little one's gray tail;
But the tails whirl faster; and once in a while
They fly round so swiftly that all in a pile
  They huddle like leaves in a gale.

There's nothing they like so well as a ball
  Of yarn all evenly wound;
Over and over they go with a rush and a fall;
One has it this time—then another—then all,
  Yarn and kittens like tops spinning round.

The old mother gray, with a face quite demure,
  Sits winking at their droll play,
And once in a while says with a purr,
"My dear little kits, you must ever prefer
  At home, with your mother to stay.

"Be senile and kind to all other cats,
  And loving to one another;
Be faithful in looking for mice and rats,
And always to dogs give spiteful pats—
  Respect and obey your mother."

Now, what will become of these kittens three
  I am sure cannot be told;
If with friends and each other they ever agree,
Then purring and mewing their lives will be
  Very happy as they grow old. — *Hearth and Home*
    The Record-Union, Sacramento, California
    Saturday, January 28, 1888, p6

Catrimony

A little girl, very much excited, rushed into the parlor, which was full of company, and exclaimed:

"Mamma, just think of it!"

"Think of what, darling?"

"Our cat has a whole lot of twins, and I didn't even know she was married!" — *Texas Siftings*

The Alma (Kansas) Signal
Saturday, December 19, 1891, p1

Natural History
In Small Chunks
for Small Children

"What is this?"

"This is a cat. Do you see the beautiful curve to his back? If you continue to be a good boy, you shall someday have a thousand cats."

"Are cats a useful animal?"

"Yes, very. If it wasn't for the cat, every house would be overrun with canary birds."

"Are cats very brave?"

"Yes. They'll hang around a corner for four hours to get their claws into a poor little mouse, not one fortieth part their size."

"What food do cats prefer?"

"A $20 mocking is their first choice. If the family are not able to keep a mockingbird, the cat must put up with an oriole or a German canary. It is only when suffering for food that a cat will accept of a sirloin steak."

"Cats can't sing, can they?"

"No, but bless 'em! They keep trying to learn how. They have got so they can sound the first four notes on the scale and they are determined to get the rest."

"What time do they sing the sweetest?"

"At night between the hours of 11 p.m. and 4 a.m. You have probably read items about bold, bad men flinging bootjacks, sticks of wood and other missiles at singing cats. Don't ever associate with such people. Cats have as much right in America as anybody else, and it is only the meanest kind of folks who will try to keep 'em from rising up in the world."

"How long do cats live?"

"Nobody knows, as no cat ever had a fair show to see how many years he could put in. After he has hung around one neighborhood for fifteen or twenty years someone murders him in cold blood."

"Does the fur of the cat contain electricity?"

"Yes, and it a great wonder why some of these scientific men did not make use of the fact in searching for the clue to the telephone. There isn't much doubt that the day will yet come when a cat in Detroit, connected by a clothes-line with one in Chicago, will form a perfect telephone line."

"Do cats suck children's breath?"

"They do. Mothers should let their children eat onions as a preventive. Plug tobacco will answer the same purpose."

The Waco (Texas) Daily Examiner
Sunday, October 27, 1878, p3

Chapter Five

Kiddy Letters

Just as frontier newspapers featured cat and kitten stories to hook young readers, the children in turn responded, either offering varied observations about mysterious felines or providing anecdotes by their interaction with cats. Some of the following excerpts were written by children while others came from adult observations. Either way, the stories reflect the curiosity of both cat and child.

No doubt cats are curious critters to children, as the felines are aloof but approachable, enigmatic yet readable, quiet but playful. As these selections indicate, boys particularly found them objects of mystery and torment. In tune with their times, boys and youth not only tormented cats but also killed them on occasion out of spite or amusement.

By the turn of the century, though, attitudes began to change with the rise of humane organizations. This transformation was exemplified in 1891 by a perplexed Galveston lad, who failed to understand the wrong he had committed in killing a cat. In a letter he signed "Tom Smith, A Boy," to the local newspaper, he wrote, "Will some just member of the (humane) society be so kind as to tell me whether it is any more permissible for the thievish cats to steal rabbits, pigeons, chickens and pet birds than it is for me to prevent such doings by killing the cats?"

Young Smith explained that cats had killed six of his rabbits, eighteen of his pigeons and twelve of his chickens. Wrote Smith, "This (humane society) member expects me to have more sympathy for two cats than for thirty-six pets," and concluded "I hope I won't be arrested."

Whether Tom Smith was arrested or not is unknown today. What is certain then as now, however, was the fascination children had for kitties as these selections show.

A Property of Cats

"Johnny, what is the name of the Australian weapon that returns when it is thrown violently forward into the air?"

"The boomerang."

"Is there anything else known to science that has that peculiar property?"

"Yes'm, the cat." — *Chicago Tribune*
The Record-Union, Sacramento, California
Tuesday, March 28, 1899, p2

A Boy's Composition on Cats

Cats don't like to swim and never do except it's an old cat that you want to get rid of and you do her up in a bag with some bricks and throw her into a mill pond off the bridge, and then she'll burst the bag and swim ashore and kite for home, so's to be there to welcome you there so's you won't feel lonesome.

Our cat lives in the house what times she don't live over to Jones barn. She is real handy to throw stones at and to pull her tail and make her squawk. I make her squawk ten or six times a day, and the backs of my hands is drawed out in lines like a map, where her toe nails has got hitched.

Cats can climb telegraph poles and set on the ridgepoles of four-story houses without being dizzy headed, and they can sleep with one eye open and lay awake with both eyes shut.

Fort Worth (Texas) Daily Gazette
Sunday, August 2, 1891, p15

Home First

We had a scrawny cat,
Afraid of mouse or rat;
So mother said one day:
"Boys, take that cat away."
We lost her in fine style
Away from home a mile.

We dropped the sack and ran
As fast as youngsters can.
How glad we were to tell

We had done out task so well!
We opened wide the door—
Our cat slept on the floor!
> *The Eugene (Oregon) Guard*
> Thursday, May 2, 1893, p3
> *The Islander*, Friday Harbor, Washington
> Thursday, September 13, 1894, p4

Johnny's Composition
He Tells About the Peculiarities of Cats

The cat is a very interesting animal. He is a small fur dog that meows, and has whiskers and several other things. He has four paws—two fore paws and two behind ones—and a tail. He has been known for many years, two of him having been said to be on the Ark, where he must have been tied up, or what would have become of the rats? Cats don't get to be cats until they are a year old, when they stop being kittens, which they are born as. It takes a kitten several weeks to get his eyes open, if he doesn't get drownded before that time, and he scratches when he is mad. My father says camels used to be cats, but got their backs up one day and couldn't get them down again, and so became camels. I never heard a camel meow, but I suppose they can, because they can do 'most anything, having seven stomachs and going many days without water.

The dictionary says a cat is a carnivorous quadruped, but that does not sound like a cat. The old Egyptians used to be very fond of the cat, treating him like a member of their own family, and making mummies out of him when he died. Some of these mummies still live. They used to hang people for killing cats in Egypt, because the cat was supposed to be a sacred animal, being a sign of the moon, probably because they are generally out all night. We have a cat named Tom, and he has six kittens, which he washes their faces every day just like me.

Cats never fall out of anything without landing on their feet, which is why their feet are so soft, and they have to be killed nine times before they die, and sometimes they don't even then. They eat milk when tame, and when wild they cry like a baby until somebody comes to see what is the matter, and then they eat him, which is fatal, and teaches people to mind their own business, and not go seeing what other people's children are crying for.

A cat's eye is a very queer thing, looking like a slot machine all day and an agate it night, seeing better in the dark than in the light, like witches. Therefore, they are said to be friends of witches, and some people don't like them on that account, but I do.

The two best cats that ever lived belonged to Dick Whittington, Mayor of London, who went out West and killed a lot of rats at a dollar a head, and took the money home to his master to get to be Mayor with, and Puss in Boots, who stole his master's clothes and ate a giant, thereby making his master owner of the farm and husband of a rich girl, whose father died and left it all to her.

My cat can't do anything like this, but he gets there just the same, and is very gentle to my little brother, who pulls his tail and doesn't have to wish he hadn't.

Altogether I don't know what we should do

without cats, especially those that like to have them lying around just as we do.

Yours truly, Johnny — *Harper's Young People*
The Record-Union, Sacramento, California
Saturday, January 23, 1892, p6

A Boy's Essay on Cats

The following is vouched for as a boy's essay on cats. It is all true, every word of it, and no doubt voices the sentiments of the average small boy everywhere in relation to the comparative merits of dogs and cats:

"I'd rather have a dog than a cat any day. Dogs can race cats; they can race other dogs; they can race boys or anything. Nobody ain't scared of a cat. A mouse is, but not if it ain't somewheres that it can't get out of, or a rat either. A dog can make a cat dead if he bites her enough. When he comes in the yard, he can make her tail look like a Christmas tree. He can make her fix her back up like a camel. I ain't afraid of thieves, but thieves are afraid of dogs. If a thief comes where a dog can get at him, he'll run like the doost; but the dog won't run. A dog can watch a house better than a policeman. He won't let the dog that owns it come in the back yard in the middle of the night; but a cat would. If a man or any other thief was to sneak in, would a cat care? She'd go over the fence like lightning. That's what. A dog knows when you're home from school. He ain't sleepy then. He has fun with old hats, if you give him one. You've got to pay for keeping him, but you don't a cat, because a dog's some good and a cat ain't. I'd rather have a dog."

The Capital Journal, Salem, Oregon
Wednesday, August 21, 1889, p1

A Remedy

"Oh, doctor, come at once, Johnnie has swallowed a mouse."

"Then the best thing you can do is to get him to swallow a cat."

The Americus (Kansas) Ledger
Friday, December 2, 1887, p2

A Boy's Composition on Cats

Cats are a great institution.

I do not know what would become of our country if there were no cats. What would little boys do if they had no cats to throw stones at, or duck in the swill tub?

What would Towser do if there were no cats to worry?

What would the hired girl do if there were no cats to account for the disappearance of pie and cake after her beau had made her a friendly call.

Cats are great lovers of music. They have also, a great deal of perseverance. They have been known to persevere for six weeks trying to pitch a tune at high G.

Cats are very strong, and can draw more than any other animal for their size. Two of them have been known to draw a boot-jack, water pitcher, shaving mug, several old shoes, a candle stick, and several pieces bedroom furniture through the window, just by the sound of their voices.

There are a great many kinds of cats. There is the black cat, white cat, gray cat, yellow cat, spotted cat, tiger cat, pole cat, cat-a-wampus, and cat-o'-nine-tails.

I know lots more about cats, but guess I will leave it till some other time. — Johnnie

The Alma (Kansas) Signal
Saturday, December 21, 1889, p2

Old Time Religion

Some of our church friends will appreciate the following from an exchange, printed at Johnson, N.Y.: A four-year-old boy is the son of strong Baptist parents. One day he tried to immerse the household cat in a bucket of water. The animal resisted. It howled, clawed and scratched. Finally, the boy with his hands covered with scratches and tears in his eyes, gave it up: "Darn you!" he said, "Go and be a Methodist if you want to!"

The Ellensburg Dawn, Ellensburg, Washington
Friday, June 16, 1899, p. 2

Retaliated on the Cat

Tommy, aged 4, wanted to sit at the dinner table one day when company was present, but was sent away with the remark that his whiskers weren't long enough for him to sit there. He was given his dinner at a small table by himself, and while he was eating a pet cat came purring about him. "Oh, go 'way," said Tommy. "Your whiskers are big enough to eat at the company table."

El Paso (Texas) Herald
Saturday, August 12, 1899, p6

Only a Boy

Only a boy, with his noise and fun,
The veriest mystery under the sun;
As brimful of mischief, and wit and glee,
As ever a human frame can be;
And as hard to manage as—what? ah me!
'Tis hard to tell, yet we love him well.

Only a boy, with his fearful trend,
Who cannot be driven, but most be led;
Who troubles the neighbors' dogs and cats,
And tears more clothes, and spoils more hats.
Loses more tops, and kites, and bats
Than would stock a store for a year or more.

Only a boy, with his wild strange ways,
With his idle hours and his busy days;
With his queer remarks, and his odd replies;
Sometimes foolish and sometimes wise;
Often brilliant, for one of his size,
As a meteor hurled from the planet-world.

Only a boy, who will be a man,
If nature goes on with its first great plan;
If water or fire, or some fatal snare.
Conspire not to rob us of this, our heir,
Our blessing, our trouble, our rest, our care,
Our torment, our joy—only a boy.

> *The Record-Union*, Sacramento, California
> Saturday, May 3, 1884, p2

Chapter Six

Cat-alists

Cats were such a part of life that they showed up on various lists posted in newspapers across the Old West. Some lists were devoted entirely to cats and others to annoyances of the day.

Some newspapers even listed felines as federal employees because some government agencies used cats to combat mice and rat problems, especially in the largest U.S. Post Offices, such as San Francisco in the 1880s and 1890s. In 1882 about a thousand of "Uncle Sam's cats," as multiple newspapers called them, were employed "to keep rats and mice from eating and destroying postal matter and canvas mail sacks." The voracious rodents "chewed holes in the sacks and thought nothing of boring clear through bags of letters in a night." Postmasters in the nation's 50 largest cities received allocations between \$8 and \$100 annually to maintain food and shelter for the feline postal inspectors.

By 1898 the *San Francisco Chronicle* was reporting that the federal government was spending "several thousand dollars annually for the maintenance of cats" at facilities such as the city's depot commissary that supplied U.S. warships along the nation's Pacific coast. "That the cats save many times their cost of support is well known, as such supplies as crackers, cheese, bacon, flour and meal are much sought after by the rodents," reported news accounts.

Newspapers frequently listed cat oddities throughout the west such as the cat that wore spectacles in San Francisco; a dog in Tombstone, Arizona, that adopted a litter of kittens after the mother died; a cat that broke up a dog fight in Lawrence, Kansas; a pussycat in Red Bluff, Oregon, that nursed a squirrel; a Miles City, Montana, cat that raised chickens; and a cat near Vinita, Oklahoma, that "has fallen very much in love" with a pet wolf.

Other cat characters appearing in local newspapers included a San Francisco cat that got drunk three times a day and another kitty in Phoenix that "if allowed will drink beer until unable to walk." A Muskogee paper reported a feline that chewed tobacco while a Wichita, Kansas, cat named "Pete" was said to play poker or at least pull in culled cards and winning pots for his gambling accomplice. The Prescott, Arizona, paper told of a railroad cat that jumped off the train at every stop to catch mice before re-boarding when the whistle blew.

Cats showed up in a lot of ways in frontier life and lists.

A Catalogue of Cats
(In Competition)

1. The cat of a sailor who braves briny billows.
2. The cat that is somehow (check) of kin to the willows.
3. The cat that I own is but part of a cat.
4. The next one is equal to nine such as that.
5. The cat that is sadly addicted to scratching.
6. The cat that is given to stealing and snatching.
7. The cat that will pinch, and it seems rather funny.
8. It sometimes is known as the cat that makes money.
9. The cat with the metal for making the same.
10. The cat this the sum will be able to name.
11. The cat that is terribly biting and sharp.
12. The cat that is noted for playing the harp.
13. The cat that takes supper, without more apology.
14. The cat that develops a taste for theology.
15. The cat that can shout, at a theater found.
16. The cat that attends to the science of sound.
17. The cat that is heavy and solid and square.
18. The cat well provided for dressing her hair,
19. The cat that is ready to tumble or drop.
20. And last is the cat that is always on top. — M.C.S.
    Galveston (Texas) Daily News
    Sunday, June 16, 1895, p13

Thankfulness

If tongues were all attached to brains,
If "hogs" were barred from railway trains,
If folks would stop at home who cough,

If empty guns would not go off,
If cats would only sleep at night,
If money would not get so tight,
If ladies' hats were less uncouth,
If weather clerks would tell the truth,
If fishermen would stick to facts,
If men would sit between the acts,
If fads and foibles were tabooed,
If death would kindly steal the dude,
How thankful we should be!

> *The Record-Union,* Sacramento, California
> Saturday, December 27, 1890, p4

Referring to the Cat

Many words, phrases and sayings refer to the cat. This name is applied to several things besides the felis. It means a short, stumpy boat (Whittiugton's cat was a cat boat), a nine-pronged lash and tackle, used to hoist the anchor on board ships. The "cat head" is the beam to which the anchor is hoisted; the cat boat a rope used near it. A "cat's nose" is a cold northeast wind; "cats' paws" are flurries on the water caused by the wind, and a "cat skin" a larger patch. There is a Hungarian proverb that a cat does not die in the water, hence its paws disturb the surface. Certain ropes on board ship are named "cat fall," "cat tail," "catharpin," and a "cats' paw" is also a kink in a rope. There is the "cat hook," the "cat block," and weak tea is called "cat lap," and a short sleep a "cat nap." A hole in the ship's quarter, through which hawsers pass, is a "cat hole," and the French apply the same

name to the "lubber hole" in the top. — F. S. Bassett
in *Globe-Democrat*
  Columbus (Nebraska) Journal
  Wednesday, June 13, 1888, p1

We Can Escape Elephants, But Gnats Never

Life is full of little worries, such for instance as:
Buying candy that is stale.
Licking a stamp that has no mucilage on it.
Getting hold of the dry lighter, in a cigar store.
Throwing away theater seat checks and keeping car
    tickets in their stead.
Trying to remember the name of the lady before you.
Clerks who snub you if you don't buy.
Cat concerts.
Howling dogs.
Newspaper not left at your door.
A sick man telling you all his complaints.
Conundrums
Bottomless Pocket.
Dry Inkstand.
Au oh! Dear, sort of a female.
People who always say yes.
Buying a thing at auction, only to see it new at less
    price in another place.
Stale eggs in omelet.
Mr. Smith, who thinks Mr. Smith the greatest man on
    earth.
Caller leaving no card or name.
Five minutes too late for excursion boat.
Wet when you want it dry.
Neck-tie too short to bow.

Collar button down trouser leg.
A screeching vocalist next door.
An old, old pun revamped.
Raspberry seed between false teeth and roof of
     mouth, at table.
A girl always hinting ice cream.
Over-shoe stuck in the mud.
Flea on your back while in church.
Iceberg feet.
Looking for rooms.
Trying to remember where you left your cane.
Corns.
Crowded car.
Parlor album, with her sisters, her cousins and her
     aunts.
Please write in album.
An over-full ash barrel.
No towel.
The man who thinks he knows you.
Smelling hartshorn for camphor.
Railway eating house pie.
Doctor bill.
Thinking of the end of it all.
     Nevada State Journal, Reno
     Saturday, May 19, 1883, p2

The Cat

Cats are curious cattle. They are selfish. They are
grasping. When the attributes were parceled out
among the animals, the catgut the gift of music. She
got it by violins.

     No one know where cats come from; but since

the fashion of seal sacques* came in, everybody knows where most of them go to. But this is kept a profound secret among the owners of seal garments. They set the seal of secrecy upon it. Perhaps they are wise.

The cat has nine lives; that is to say, she lives nine times longer than she ought.

This suggests a problem, which lovers of mathematics—there are those, alas! who love them—can puzzle over. If it takes nine tailors to make one live man, and nine lives to make one cat, what does a catamount do? (Correspondents sending answers will please enclose a three-cent stamp, not for publication, but for the use of the compiler of this authentic history.)

The cat is not subject to tax. Efforts have been made to insert a clause in the dog law to include cats, but thus far the cats have inserted their own claws.

Not only do they escape tax, but the taxidermist also. They do their own stuffing.

At the time of the flood Father Noah endeavored to keep the cat out of the ark, but the cat got her back up and passed under the guise of a camel.

Until very recently every ship since that time carried a cat.

Many stories are told of the seafaring cat, including nine tails, which are often red.

In Egypt cats were regarded as sacred animals. To kill one was an offense punishable with death.

The cat remembers this, and to this day takes a fence on the slightest provocation.

Formerly when a cat died all the inmates of the house went into mourning. Now the household go out into the night and erect bootjacks to its memory. They don't wait till morning.

The Egyptians worshipped a cat-headed deity, and marines, who cling to old superstitions, still set up cat-heads in their ships.

The Egyptian cat lived in a dark age; the modern closes her existence in a sausage.

Catskins were a favorite trimming in the Middle Ages, whence arose the proverb a skinned cat is better than it looks.

The cat's kin are exclusively used as a trimming for back fences.

A catkin is a young cat, and is great on the spring. In the spring she may be seen among the topmost branches of the willows.

Cats were introduced into England from the island of Cyprus. They are not found in the cypress now; only on willows.

In ancient Wales a cat fetched the same price as a calf. Her modern wails now frequently fetch a whole cowhide in the shape of boot leather.

Cats are Baptists by profession, but those who indulge their predilection during the early kittenhood seldom survive.

Cats do not open their eyes until nine days old. Do they ever close them again? Nein. Throw a bootjack at a sleeping cat and you will be convinced of this.

Cats are supposed to be accomplices of witches, which is probably "because they love the darkness rather than light.

Cat are very mewsical. They are all base singers. The nocturnal is their favorite composition.

Nox is their especial deity. Knocks always

accompany their concerts.

It is said that cats are cleverer than dogs and more easily trained. They are great pedestrians, and can make more laps in a given time than any other animal.

They are very courageous, and always come up to the scratch.

They are very frugal. You have seen them chasing their tails in their endeavors to make both ends meet.

They are fond of winter amusement. You remember what the New England Primer says, "the cat doth play, and after sleigh."

They are generally healthy, notwithstanding we hear of "the cat ill upon a thousand hills."

A great many more things might be said about the cat.

But silent be. It is the cat!

*a short jacket that fastens at the neck
Santa Cruz (California) Weekly Sentinel
Saturday, May 21, 1881, p4

Superstitions about Cats

In the Tyrol, girls who are fond of cats marry early.

Throwing a cat overboard from a ship will cause a cyclone.

The Pennsylvania Dutch believe black cats cure epilepsy.

Three drops of a black cat's blood is said to be a cure for croup.

If a cat washes herself calmly and smoothly, the weather will be fair.

If the family cat lies with its back to the fire, there will be a squall.

A person who despises cats will be carried to his grave in a howling storm.

If a cat sneezes three times the whole family will soon suffer from influenza.

To dream of a black cat at Christmas time in Germany is an omen of alarming illness.

If it rains on a Dutch girl's wedding day, it is because the bride has forgotten to feed her cat.

In Ireland the cat must not be taken to a new house by a moving family, especially if water has to be crossed.

A cat born in May will be of a melancholy disposition, given to catching snakes and bringing them into the house.

If it rains when there is a large washing on the line in Germany, it is a sure sign that the house mother has ill-treated the cat.

Bad luck will follow if a black cat crosses your path, for the devil prowls about, especially at night, in the guise of a black cat.

In Scotland they used to cure erysipelas by cutting off half a cat's ear and letting the blood from the wound drop on the diseased part.

In moving in Scotland, the family cat is thrown into the new house before the family enters in order that it may absorb any disease or curse left by the former tenants.

Arizona Daily Star, Tucson, Arizona
Saturday, November 7, 1896, p4

Chapter Seven

Catsop's Fables and Tales

Fables contribute to a literary genre of longstanding across multiple cultures around the world. In western culture, Aesop's Fables are likely the best known. Written by a storyteller in Greek bondage some six centuries B.C., the fables have endured because of their lasting values and moral lessons they have illustrated. Aesop's fables involving felines include *The Cat and the Mice* and *Venus and the Cat*.

Fables and other stories and poems about cats showed up regularly in Old West newspapers, sometimes directed at children and other times at all readers. Because of the interest in cats, printers likely kept some stories on the subject in reserve for filler when the news of the day or week failed to fill the news hole as the same cat stories regularly appeared in various editions of the newspaper.

Of all the fables, parables and stories of cats, perhaps the most prevalent was that of the cats of

Kilkenny, two felines from County Kilkenny, Ireland. The pair despised each other so much that they fought until their unlikely but mutual demise by consuming each other whole. The antagonistic cats became a frequent 19th century simile for opponents involved in a conflict likely to destroy them both. Hundreds of references to the Kilkenny cats peppered Old West papers—and those elsewhere in the United States—whenever a major dispute arose, whether it was between railroad magnates, political parties or local candidates.

When lessons were to be taught or morals instilled, cats were often used by pioneer journalists to get the message across.

A Verse about the Kilkenny Cats

Someone has put the story of the Kilkenny cats into verse as follows:

"There wonst was two cats at Kilkenny,
And each thought there was one cat too many;
And they scratched and they spit
And they fought and they bit;
Till excepting their tails.
And some scraps of their nails.
Instead of two cats, there wan't any."
The Coffeyville (Kansas) Daily Journal
Monday, June 4, 1894, p3

The Dog and the Cat
A Fable

A dog sat howling in a yard and a black cat sat on the wall.

"Why do you make such a noise?" asked the cat; "are you howling at me? If so, I will go at once, as I do not wish to annoy you."

"Howling at you, indeed," replied the dog. "No, I scarcely saw you. I am howling at the moon."

"Why?"

The dog was silent for a moment, and then he answered. "I don't know. I've always howled at the moon, and my father and mother did, and so did their fathers and mothers, and therefore I do the same?"

"What harm has the moon done to you?" asked the cat.

"Not any that I know of?" replied the dog, "excepting that when it is night and ought to be dark the moon shines out and makes it light. I suppose I don't like things being turned upside down. At any rate I have howled at the moon ever since I was a puppy, and I suppose I always shall. It's my nature— one can't help one's nature."

"Ah," said the cat, "you should get rid of such ways. And as for saying it's your nature, all I can say that the sooner you get rid of nature the better. It only requires a little determination."

And the cat purred complacently.

"Now I like a moonlight night," said she, "the rabbits come out and play and frisk about, and I can pounce upon one at once and carry it off."

"Poaching," answered the dog gravely, "that is a bad habit, I'm sure—stealing in fact. And there's no occasion for it—you have your saucer of milk in the morning and evening, and a fine dish of scraps for dinner, so you have not the excuse of hunger. Why don't you give up poaching?"

"Oh, that would be impossible," said the cat, with a simper; "you know it's a cat's nature to poach, it is a thing not to be resisted. When one thinks of the number of delicious young rabbits, what can one do but to make an expedition in their direction?—and when one sees them, why, it is hopeless to war against one's nature. It is impossible."

"Impossible," said the dog, slyly, "no not impossible."

"Quite," answered the cat decidedly.

"Ah, then," said the dog, "you do not get rid of old practice any more than I do. You can't go against your nature any more than I can against mine. Ah, madam, it is very easy to reprove others and point out to them the error of their ways; but it is not so easy to reform one's self, and take to new habits. I suppose I shall go on howling at the moon, and you will go on poaching as long as we are dog and cat."

The cat looked disconcerted for a moment and then she leaped down on the other side of the wall.

The dog shook his head. "Ah," said he, "that is getting rid of her nature, is it? She's gone off to poach by the light of the moon, and as she cannot answer my arguments, she feels it is the best thing to say nothing at all. Very wise of you Mrs. Cat, but I hope you will in future not attempt to mend the ways of others until you can mend your own. — *Little Folks*

The Head Light, Thayer, Kansas
Friday, January 29, 1886, p7
The Schuyler (Nebraska) Sun

Thursday, February 11, 1886, p6
The Lyons (Kansas) Republican
Thursday, February 18, 1886, p3

The Suicidal Cat
A Fable

There was a man named Ferguson,
  He lived on Market Street,
He had a speckled Thomas cat,
  That couldn't well be beat;
He'd catch more rats and mice and such
  Than forty cats could eat.

This cat would come into the room
  And climb upon a cheer,
And there he'd sit and lick hisself
  And purr so awful queer,
That Ferguson would yell at him —
  But still he'd purr-severe

And then he'd climb the moonlit fences,
  And loaf around and yowl,
And spit and claw another cat
  Alongside of the jowl;
And then they both would shake their tails
  And jump around and howl.

Oh, this here cat of Ferguson's
  Was fearful then to see;
He'd yell precisely like he was
  In awful agony;

You'd think a first-class stomach-ache
  Had struck some small baby.

And all the mothers in the street
  Waked by the horrid din,
Would rise right up and search their babes,
  To find some worryin' pin;
And still this vigorous cat would keep
  A hollerin' like sin.

And as for Mr. Ferguson,
  'Twas more than he could bear
And so he hurled his bootjack out
  Right through the midnight air;
But this vociferous midnight cat,
  Not one cent did he care.

For still he yowled and kept his fur
  A standin' upon end,
And his old spine a-doublin' up
  As far as it would bend,
As if his hopes of happiness
  Did on his lungs depend.

But while a curvin' of his spine,
  And waiting to attack
A cat upon the other fence,
  There came an awful crack;
And this here speckled Thomas cat
  Was busted in the back

When Ferguson came down next day
  There lay his old feline,
And not a life was left in him,

Although he had had nine;
"All this has come," said Ferguson,
   "Of curvin' of his spine."

Now all ye men whose tender hearts
   This painful tale does rack,
Just take this moral to yourselves,
   All of you, white and black;
Don't ever go like this here cat,
   To gettin' up your back!
         The Carson Daily Appeal, Carson City, Nevada
         Friday, March 13. 1868, p3
         The Galveston (Texas) Daily News
         Saturday, March 21, 1868, p4

A Fable

A silly mouse, thinking each thing a cat,
Fell into helpless worriment thereat;

But, noticed by a wizard living near,
Was turned into a cat to end its fear.

No sooner was the transformation done
Than dreadful terror of a dog begun.

Now when the wizard saw this latest throe,
"Here, be a dog," he said, "and end your woe."

But, though a dog, its soul had no release,
For fear some tiger might disturb its peace.

Into a tiger next the heart was made,
And still 'twas fretful and sore afraid,

Because the huntsman might some ill-starred day
Happen along and take its life away.

"Then," said the wizard, turning to his house,
"You have a mouse's heart—now be a mouse."

'Tis so with men; no earthly help or dower
Can add one atom to their native power.

Them from their smallness nothing can arouse;
No art can make a lion from a mouse."
    Aberdeen (Washington) Herald
    Thursday, August 25, 1892, p4

To "Prowl," My Cat

You are life's true philosopher,
  An epicure of air and sun,
An egoist in sable fur,
  To whom all moralists are one.

You hold your race traditions fast—
  While others toil, you simply live,
And based upon a staple past,
  Remain a sound conservative!

You see the beauty of the world
  Through eyes of unalloyed content,
And, in my study chair upcurled,
  Move me to pensive wonderment!

I wish I knew your trick of thought,
  The perfect balance of your ways.
They seem an inspiration caught
  From other laws in older days.

Your padded footsteps prowl my room
  Half in delight and half disdain;
You like this air of studious gloom
  When streets without are cold with rain!

Someday, alas! you'll come to die
  And I shall lose a constant friend;
You'll take your last look at the sky
  And be a puzzle to the end! — C.K.B. in *London
Spectator*
      The Alma (Kansas) Signal
      Saturday, January 5, 1895, p4
      The Record-Union, Sacramento, California
      Saturday, February 16, 1895, p8

False Kindness

The softest little fluff of fur!
The gentlest, most persuasive purr!
Oh, everybody told me that
She was the "*loveliest* little cat!"
So when she on the table sprung,
And lapped the cream with small red tongue,
I only gently put her down,
And said, "no, no!" and tried to frown;
But if I had been truly kind
I should have made that kitten mind!

Now, large and quick, and strong of will,
She'll spring upon the table still,
And, spite of all my watchful care,
Will snatch the choicest dainties there;
And everybody says, "Scat! scat!
She's such a dreadful, *dreadful* cat!"
But I, who hear them, know, with shame,
I only am the one to blame,
For in the days when she was young,
And lapped the cream with small red tongue,
Had I to her been truly kind
I should have made that kitten mind. — Marion
      Douglas, in *Harper's Young People.*
      The Record-Union, Sacramento, California
      Saturday, August 27, 1892, p7

The Catastrophe of a Masher

A tom-cat sat on a backyard fence
With an aching heart and a soul intense,
Rigged out in style in every sense
     Immense.

He sat alone in his faultless attire,
And his bosom burned with a sacred fire
As he watched for his love, his only desire—
     Maria

He was musing upon his lonely lot,
And he said to himself, "She cometh not,
What a terrible heartache I have got—
     Great Scott!

How terribly lonesome I feel! How queer
To be sitting alone with nobody near—
O, how much I wish Maria was here—
  Mon Dieu!

"The thought of it fills me with horrible doubt—
I should smile, I should blush, I should wail, I should
  shout,
Just suppose some fellow had cut me out—
  Me-out!

"Ah, there she comes now, as soft a rat;"
But alas! He'd mistaken the soft pit-a-pat,
His Maria was only a brother tom-cat—
  How's that?"

Thought Tom No. 1 of Tom No. 2.
But No. 2 bounced him without more ado,
And suddenly both departed from view—
  Mew! Mew!

Oh, ill fared it then for Tom No. 1,
For as soon as the enemy's work was done
Of all his fine raiment he left him none—
  Such fun!

Now, all you young mashers who dress with such
  care,
The hearts of the guileless to slave and ensnare
You'd better remember this tale and beware—
  Take care.
  Arizona Silver Belt, Globe Gila, Arizona
  Saturday, March 24, 1883, p1

Why Cats Wash After Eating

You may have noticed, little friends,
  That cats don't wash their faces
Before they eat, as children do,
  In all good Christian places.

Well, years ago, a famous cat,
  The pangs of hunger feeling,
Had chanced to catch a fine young mouse
  Who said, as he ceased squealing:

"All genteel folks their faces wash
  Before they think of eating!"
And, wishing to be thought well-bred,
  Puss heeded his entreating.

But when she raised her paw to wash,
  Chance for escape affording,
The sly young mouse said his good-bye
  Without respect to wording.

A feline council met that day,
  And passed in solemn meeting,
A law forbidding any cat
  To wash till after eating. — *Outlook*
    Weekly Oregon Statesman, Salem, Oregon
    Friday, September 8, 1899, p3
    Abilene (Kansas) Daily Chronicle
    Wednesday, December 20, 1899, p4

The Outcasts

In attic high and grim and scant,
  A ragged creature lonely sat.
His face was lined by pain and want—
At once he cried "Begone! avaunt!"
  As o'er the threshold crept a cat.

"Stay, stranger, do not drive me hen
  I pray thee list my tale of woe;
I am too poor to give offense,
And, lacking now in every sense,
  I scarce fear either word or blow.

"It was not always thus; before
  They drove me for the streets to roam
I always found an open door—
Alas, when we grow old and poor
  That we should be without a home!

"The children loved to stroke my back,
  When I was sleek and round and fat—
Make fly the sparks and list them crack,
They called me pretty puss. Alack!
  I'm now but a neglected cat!

"Once when a bell the children found—
  A tiny, tinkling bell—they tied
It with a pretty ribbon round
My neck, and at its merry sound
  They laughed and laughed until they cried.

Today, whene'er my form they spy,
  With ready hand they fling the bat

And I am forced for life to fly;
I've lost a foot—an ear—an eye;
  There is no pity for a cat.

"My teeth are gone, my claws are dulled,
  I cannot hope to take a rat;
The hair from off my back is pulled—
My fare from backyard garbage culled—
  Alas! I am a sorry cat."

"Poor creature, you have come at last
  To one who feels your woe; I like you,
By all the heartless world outcast,
I dream of an embittered past
  That proved all false I once thought true.

Come, maimed and ragged as you are,
  Take half my crust; 'tis hard and dry
And all I have—but you shall share;
And while I live, so you shall fare
  "Till one or both of us shall die!" — Charles E.
Banks in *Arkansas Traveler*
    Daily Capital Journal, Salem, Oregon
    Friday, January 3, 1890, p2

A Love Match

Little Miss Pussy cat sat in the closet,
  As white as a pure flake of snow;
Old Mistress Pussy cat slept in the sunshine,
  And blinked now and then in its glow.
There crept through the hedge a feline marauder,
  Seeking perchance a wife to wed;

Bearing so stately, mien so uncommon,
  Kitty was captured heart and head.
They purred and they languished till Pussy awoke,
  Who saw at a glance the danger;
With proper decorum and matronly airs
  She asked the name of the stranger.
"Thomas Grimalkin," bold spoke the intruder.
  "I come from my home for a bride."
"Sir Thomas Grimalkin, I think?" said the dame;
  And how her green eyes opened wide.
"No, no, Madam Tabby, I am not a sir,
  Nor boast I my blood's azure hue;
As Thomas Grimalkin your daughter I seek
  As Thomas Grimalkin I sue."
Then up in an instant rose Tabitha's back;
  "No plain Mister Thomas for me,
For only with rank my Katrina shall wed,
  Or else she a spinster shall be.
Already, thrice over, her hand I've refused
  To knights of the Order of Malta,
For no one with less than a baronet's rank
  Shall lead Katrina to the altar."
But fancy her horror to see little Kate,
  Defiant, at once turn the tide.
"My mother can wait for Sir Thomas," she said,
  "But you can have me for your bride."
"This changes the case," Grimalkin now spoke,
  "Since you plain Thomas will marry,
We will hie to the church at once to be wed,
  Not even an hour to tarry."
Miss Kitty dropped low on her knees in the grass,
  "Forgive me, dear mother," she said,
"You know I must marry the one of my choice,
  If I would be happy when wed."

Grimalkin stood near, and looked very grave,
  Till he saw the mother relent;
Then he gave her his card, and on it she read:
  "Lord Thomas Grimalkin, of Kent." — *London Society*

    The Record-Union, Sacramento, California
    Saturday, December 8, 1888, p7

Chapter Eight

Purr-pose and Hiss-story

Since cats were first domesticated in the Middle East close to a hundred centuries ago, men and women have attempted to understand the fickle felines. Those efforts have been largely unsuccessful due to the aloofness and independence of the breed. The mysterious temperaments of cats intrigued and amused 19th century residents of the American West just as they do contemporary Americans, seeking to understand their furry friends.

An enduring question throughout the centuries has always been what is the purpose of a cat's life? Was it to serve humanity? Or, more likely, to be attended by man, woman and child? That question was asked by pioneers and likely answered the same then as today with cats triumphant.

Because of the enigmatic nature of cats, they fascinated westerners—at least during the daylight hours—and provided reading material in their newspapers, which printed stories on feline history and folk tales. If the frequency of stories is a true indication, pioneers were especially intrigued by the veneration of cats as deities by the ancient Egyptians as such stories were regularly featured in Old West news journals.

Good Investment

Trouble and kin and cats are about the only things a man can have that other people don't try to get away from him.

The Advocate, Lakin, Kansas
Thursday, November 24, 1892, p3

How Cats Regard Men
Think Human Beings Were Created for Their Especial Benefit

The cat was a solitary roamer, whose companions were the trees of its native forests. It found a home in the hollow trunks and safety among the branches. How do we know that the cat's ancestors were dwellers in the forests? Because every kitten takes to a tree as readily as a duck to water. Also, because nearly all forest dwellers are mottled in color, so that they may not be conspicuous among the light and shadows beneath the trees.

While I was considering what was the probable view held by cats about human beings, it was suggested by one ingenious friend that probably they regard a man as a kind of locomotive tree, pleasant to rub against the lower limbs of which afford a comfortable seat, and from whose upper branches occasionally drop tidbits of mutton and other luscious fruits. We may laugh at the theory, but it has quite a respectable string of facts behind it to buck it up. If the Kanakas argued from the pig to the horse, why should not the cat pass from the familiar tree to the unfamiliar organization called man? The cat, in spite of the domestic character it has acquired, is in reality the least tamed of our animal servants. As far as its duties are concerned, man has taught it practically nothing.

The Bryan (Texas) Daily Eagle
Thursday, January 7, 1897, p2

Cat Legends
The Animal First Appeared
With Noah in the Ark.

In Arabian legends the cat is traced back as far as Noah and the ark. It is one of the animals that came off the ark, but did not go on. When the other creatures entered for safety during the time when "the doors of heaven were to be opened and the fountains of the deep turned loose," there was no cat among them. Puss' origin is accounted for in this way: During the time the ark was floating about over the tall mountains, mice and rats became an intolerable nuisance to the people on the great vessel, and they complained to Noah that everything was being literally devoured by the pesky vermin. That august personage forthwith called the male lion to his side and began to stroke his back, whereupon the great beast sneezed and lo a full-sized cat was blown from his nostrils!

The ancient Greeks thought that all creatures except rats had souls and that that animal lost its soul through a bargain made between a bridge architect and the devil. The architect had besought the devil to get his help in constructing an exceedingly dangerous bridge structure and his Satanic Majesty only consented to lend aid on condition that the first creature to cross it should lose its soul. This was agreed upon, the bridge finished in due time and the devil sent to the opposite side to await his prey. The shrewd architect took good care to send a cat over before any human being was allowed to cross. On learning of the bargain, the cat re-crossed the bridge and scratched the architect's eyes out

The titular deity of cats was Diana, and, according to Plutarch, the cat was not only sacred to the moon, but was an emblem of it. Hence cats were treated with peculiar consideration in the land of the Pharaohs, the death of one being regarded as the greatest family misfortune. Egyptian cat funerals were celebrated with the greatest pomp and ceremony, their late owners showing respect by shaving off their eyebrows and wearing sackcloth for nine days. In the time of Moses, it was a capital crime to kill a cat, and we are told by Diodorus how a Roman soldier who killed one was tried, sentenced and finally put to death.

The Evening Kansan, Newton, Kansas
Saturday, September 17, 1892, p3

The Cat in Folk Lore
Prominent in the Mythology of the Earliest Nations

The cat has figured in folk lore and popular superstitions more than any other animal, except perhaps the serpent, and is prominent in the mythology of the earliest nations. In Egypt, especially, it was regarded with peculiar veneration, or with superstitious fear. The presence of thousands of mummies of cats testify to this adoration of the feline tribe. The ancient "Book of the Dead" speaks of Mau, the Great Cat, meaning the sun—the eye of that animal glowing and contracting in the light, being taken to represent the orb of day. The feline tribe is also prominent in India.

As an instrument of power in the hands of Satan and his witch subjects, the cat would naturally become a weather maker. Its early connection with Diana, the moon goddess, would also indicate the same power over the elements possessed by that orb. Witches frequently used it to raise storms. The cat is particularly regarded with distrust by sailors, who say: "It carries a gale in its tail," and that it will surely provoke a storm to throw one overboard. Even while on board, if it is unusually frolicsome, a gale of wind is thought to be imminent. Many stories are told of storms caused by the sacrifice of a cat. These animals are said to smell a wind, while pigs see it. This storm raising power is not confined to witches' familiars, nor to cats at sea.

The cat is universally weatherwise. In the west of Ireland, you may obtain a good wind by burying a cat up to its neck in sand on the seashore, with its head opposite to the desired direction. There is an old story told in Block Island of a man who shut a cat up in a barrel to prevent a hostile skipper from sailing, and no fair wind came until pussy was released. In Lancashire, stormy and wet weather is coming when puss frisks about the house. In Ireland, if she stretches so that her paws touch, bad weather will ensue. Scotch fishermen declare that if she sneezes or licks her paws, rain will surely come. In Shetland, the cat "gaanin in da luft" foretells wind, and "sleepin' on her harns" (with the back of her head down) indicates calms. An old English writer says: "When the cat washes her face over the ears, we shall have great store of rain."

A German proverb says, "If the cat basks in the sun in February she will go back to the stove in March." "Cats courting the fire," says the author of *Nature's Secrets*, "more than ordinary, or licking their feet and trimming the hair of their head and mustaches, prognosticates rainy weather." In our own country if the cat sneezes, it is a sign of rain; if it snores, of foul weather. When cats wash themselves, fair weather is coming, unless the face is washed over the ear, in which case foul weather is imminent, and rain if it is the head behind the ears.

If pussy washes her face after a rain, wind will come from the point to which she turns, and a thaw will occur if she washes her face with her back to the fire in winter. Rain is also indicated when the cat scratches itself, a storm when it claws chair or table legs, lies on its head with its mouth open, or sits tail toward the fire. A change of weather is indicated by the electrification of the cat's fur, and wind is coming when her tail is bushy and stiff.

The presence of the cat in the house is usually deemed an omen of good luck. "Who has a cat has a happy married life," says a German proverb. In antiquity omens were I drawn from the entrance and exit of strange cats, and it was then a bad sign to have a cat cross your path. This is still believed in many places. In Ireland persons entering a house say, "God save all here except the cat." And if anyone, in setting out upon a journey, should meet a cat and look it squarely in the face, the journey must be postponed. It is also an ill omen for a cat to cross your path when you first go out in the morning. In Sussex, if the cat sneezes she must be summarily ejected from the house, for three such explosions would bring misfortune upon the family.

The cat has figured extensively in nursery lore. The well-known tale of "Puss in Boots" has been recognized in the popular tales of many countries widely separated. In Japan the Wind God is figured with a cat's face and claws, and in China wooden cats adorn the ridges of the houses to ward off storms and tempests. The Irish say there is [a] king of the cats who may be discovered by nipping off a bit of his ear. He will then speak and declare his authority.

The cat in folk lore is commonly diabolical, and in the bag of proverbs has probably a diabolical allusion. The popular idea that it has nine lives expresses its mystical character. — F. S. Bassett in *Globe-Democrat*

Pullman (Washington) Herald
Friday, July 10, 1891

Asked and Answered

We have homing pigeons, why not a breed of homing cats. Nonsense, Mr. P! Not so! It's sense. The festive tom and tabby are naturally homing stock. Nothing is more so, nothing clings closer to home, be it ever so humble. Nothing will get back to its own back-yard quicker than a cat when kidnapped and carried to the land of strangers. Why, then, should not the toms and tabbies leave their animated moonlight debates and come down to business? See how many miles they can run in a specified time. Say a minute and a half. Oh, but a cat can run, when it feels like it, take Mr. P's word for that.

If you don't consider that Mr. P's word has any established market value, then take the following as proof of the fact. At Lutuch, Germany, 37 able-bodied, mild-eyed, sinewy cats were put into bags and taken 24 miles from the city. They were turned loose at 2 o'clock one afternoon. Each cat on being released lifted up its nose, sniffed the strange air, realized that it was away from home, and, in the language of the common people, proceeded to "get thar Eli." The winner of the race reached its home forty-three minutes past six that afternoon, and within twenty-four hours every cat of the 37 had run the gauntlet of dogs and small boys, and was washing the dust of the journey from its feline face as it sat at home again on its back-yard fence.

Homing cats? Well now Mr. P.— would smile, so to speak. — Joseph Pinafeather in *Fanciers Monthly*
The Abilene (Texas) Reporter
Friday, May 1, 1891, p6

Why Cats Hiss

Why does a cat hiss when angry? Take a tiny kitten at play and make it angry and it will snarl in its baby fashion and hiss as best it can. Why? In *Pearson's Magazine* Dr. Louis Robinson says that the hissing and spitting of young kittens is probably an instinctive attempt to scare away enemies from the helpless tots by imitating a snake's hiss. A great many creatures that live in shallow holes have a like habit of hissing when annoyed or angered. The tail of a cat seen dimly in the half light of a cave suggests a snake's tail and is often marked in a way to heighten the resemblance. "If," says Dr. Robinson, "this really is an instance of protective mimicry, I think it is probable that the chief foe guarded against was the eagle. Eagles are very fond of cat flesh, and it has been remarked by naturalists that these formidable birds habitually make war upon the smaller felidae."

The Alma (Kansas) Signal
Saturday, December 2, 1899, p8

Very Natural History
An Exceedingly Mew-ving Essay
on the Cat and Her Habits

I am going to write this article for my own amusement and to fill up space. My editor objects to natural history anecdotes, but I feline know more about the cat this week than anything else, so I am preparing this item on purpose.

It has been hinted in well-informed circles that the cat is a quadruped, because, forsooth, it has four feet, but any such claim is four-feeted when we remember that every yard contains at least one cat at night, and a yard is only three feet.

How cats originated is only known to the promoters of the scheme; but they are indigenous to roofs, back fences and vacant lots, and command considerable attention from the community at large and small. It is believed that the earlier settlers came from Kamscatka, while other accounts assert that Catalonia was their native country.

Cats are omnivorous, carnivorous, graminivorous and the rest of the ivorouses. They kill mice and rats, and some people have seen Catskill mountains, but this statement is as old as the hills themselves.

Cats are of two brands, the Tom and the Tabby, and there used tabby a third species, called "cat-o'-nine-tails," but this is being regularly used up—at the penitentiary.

Although the cat is called a domestic animal, it is not quite so useful as a horse or a cow, but a cattle furnish more music than either of the larger quadrupeds. And its hearers get more mew sick, too.

The power that an average cat has over the ordinary human being is remarkable. I have known men to lie awake at night and listen to the impromptu duets of a Tom and Tabby, listen to the soul-stirring melody of an inspired nocturne, and, in the wilderness of their enthusiasm, lacking the prescribed floral tribute to merit, throw to the performers their bootjacks, boots and even chamber crockery. I have known men to do this. I have seen them do it. I have done it myself.

It has been said, and truly, that a cat has nine lives, and this is one powerful reason why insurance companies can never be got to insure the life or lives of pussy. If you ask them to do so they say it is impussyble.

And yet, "to what base uses may we yet return?" A cat, when really dead for the ninth and last time of asking, is not only used for base purposes but for fiddlers also, and it must bow to circumstances.

If would be a violinsinuation to say that it did not do its duty as well in death as in life, and if anyone familiar with the midnight pleadings of a favorite tom-cat should listen to the alleged music of an amateur violinist and not recognize the affinity between their respective performances, that man or woman is dead to the wonderful coincidences of nature. — *Texas Siftings*

The Record-Union, Sacramento, California
Monday, August 6, 1888, p4

Power of the Press

Newspaper borrowers—May theirs be a life of single blessedness—may their paths be carpeted with cross-eyed snakes, and their nights be haunted by knock-kneed tom-cats!

Boon's Lick Times, Fayette, Missouri
Saturday, March 26, 1842, p3
Glasgow (Missouri) Weekly Times
Thursday, May 4, 1854, p2

Neither Republicat nor Democat

Cats have no fixed political belief. They're usually on the fence.

> *Arizona Daily Star*, Tucson, Arizona
> Sunday, December 7, 1879, p1

Cat Tails and Tales

If you will take one cat by himself and pinch his tail he will scratch and bite your hand. But take two cats and put them side by side and pinch both their tails at the same time and they will bite and scratch each other.

So it gets the people arrayed in two old parties and then pinches their tails and they fight each other. Like the cats, they never turn to fight the hand that is pinching them. — *Kaufman Leader*

> *Appeal to Reason*, Girard, Kansas
> Saturday, November 6, 1897

Matronly Outlook

The Old lady who keeps cats seems to have a purr-puss in life. — *Life*

> *The Weekly Chieftain*, Vinita, Oklahoma
> Thursday, October 20, 1887, p4

A Great Truth

Some men are like cats. You may stroke the fur the right way for years and hear nothing but purring; but accidentally tread on the tail, and all memory of former kindness is obliterated.

Weekly Oregon Statesman, Salem, Oregon
Tuesday, July 15, 1856, p1

Rule to Live By

Here is what good cats do:
"They meditate much upon the doings of rats,
And never frisk about like other bad cats."

The San Saba (Texas) Weekly News
Friday, January 8, 1892, p1

City and Country Cats
Many Curious Points of Difference

An observer has noted that there exist many points of difference between country and city cats. The country cats, he declares, are larger and heavier than those of the city, no reference being made in this comparison to such civic cats as might come under the head of "pampered pets," but only to plain cats—the cats of the back yard and the housetop. This superior weight of the country cat, the observer says, is easily attributable to the diet of small field animals and birds which it enjoys. But there are other peculiarities of difference, he proceeds, which are not so easily attributable to diet. For instance, the color of the country cat is generally either gray or tortoise shell, the commoner color being gray. On the other hand, observes the cat expert, the preponderating color among city cats is black.

In the next place the color of the eyes in city and country cats is found to be very different, the latter leaning largely to gray and green, while the city cats' eyes are mostly yellow and having far more glitter in them than have their country cousins. In the matter of tails, too, there is a difference, the city cat's tail being much longer and carried more nearly on a level with the back than that of the country eat. The country cat's paws are much flatter, broader and softer than the town cat's, the pads of the former being like velvet, and those of the latter like rubber.

Altogether, between the big-barreled gray, light eyed, velvet footed country cat, slipping noiselessly through the young wheat stalks, and the scrawny, long tailed, yellow-eyed city cat pattering down an alleyway like a flying shadow, there are such differences as will, says the observer, result in time in the formation of two distinct species *Felis rusticus* and *Felis urbanis.* — *New York Sun*

The Eugene (Oregon) Guard
Monday, May 13, 1895, p3

All Kinds of Cats; Here Are the Best

Those who are contemplating investing in cats might study this to advantage.

A good cat—the kind you want to have around the house will have a round, stubby, pug nose, fat cheeks and full upper lip, and a well-developed bump on top of the head and between the ears, betokening good nature. A sleepy cat, one that purrs a good deal, is apt to be playful and good natured.

Avoid a cat with thin, sharp nose and twitching ears.

A great mistake is in over-feeding domestic cats with too much meat. If they are over fed, they will become lazy, and will not catch mice. Overfeeding also leads to stomach troubles and "fits."

Abilene (Kansas) Daily Reflector
Tuesday, September 5, 1889, p2

About Cats

Nobody has ever been able to utilize cats, except the ancient Egyptians and spinsters. The former reverenced them, and erected temples to their worship. The latter tolerates them because she can't get anything better to tolerate.

Cat statistics have never been given that careful degree of attention by the government that their prominence in the household entitles them to, and the census reports are bare of facts relating to them, so that it is impossible to procure reliable data for the instruction of the public upon this interesting topic. It is believed, however, that there is an average of three cats to every household in Texas. There were, in 1880, 258,562 households in the state, and this, by a simple mathematical calculation, on the basis assumed, allows us a wealth of 762,686 cats. They are divided into two classes, the tom-cat and pussy-cat.

The cat is a gregarious animal, and is much addicted to holding political conventions, where the parliamentary models of Greenback political bodies prevail in their deliberations and discussions. Their native modesty—the cat's, of course, not the Greenbackers'—causes them to prefer the silence of night and the seclusions of back yards for their meetings. It is believed, from the earnestness of their demonstrations, that the majority of attendants at these meetings are aldermen in the cat municipality. Their conduct is often quite aldermanic, and the remarks they address to each other sound very much like aldermanic language.

In the absence of reliable statistics upon which to proceed to generalization, we hazard the guess that the 762,686 cats in Texas attract nightly more than 250,000 old boots, blacking-brushes, boot-blacks and other convenient missiles.

The preliminary statement in this article that the utilization of cats was confined to but two parties is incorrect. Upon reflection we recollect that the energetic small boy frequently finds a field for the use of cats. He selects two, usually of the tom class, and attaches them securely to each other by the terminal appendages that they have thoughtfully provided for that purpose, then suspends them from a pole beneath the bedroom window of some nervous old gentleman, whom their symphonies soon lull to rest—in some other part of the building. Cats and small boys are much addicted to this kind of recreation.

It is a popular delusion that cats have nine lives, though it is a well-established scientific truth that some of them have nine tails. This class flourish[es] most on board ships.

Fort Worth (Texas) Daily Gazette
Thursday, September 27, 1883, p4

Habits of the Cat
The Actions Show
It Is a Solitary Animal by Nature and Free from Greediness

All the cat's habits show it to be by nature a solitary animal. Even in early life, when family ties bring out the instinct of association, this is apparent. If you compare the play of puppies with that of kittens you will find in one case companionship of some kind is an essential, for if a puppy has no playmate of his own species, he will try to make use of the nearest biped; whereas a cork or a bit of string is all that is necessary to satisfy the requirements of the kitten. The way in which the cat takes its food is a sure sign that in its natural state it is not in the habit of associating with greedy companions, says Wild Traits in Tame Animals.

When given something to eat it first carefully smells the morsel, then takes it in a deliberate and gingerly way and sits down to finish it at leisure. There is none of that inclination to snatch hastily at any food held before it which we observe even in well-trained dogs; nor does a cat seem in any hurry to stow its goods in one place where thieving rivals cannot interfere with them. Indeed, no greater contrast in natural table manners can be observed anywhere than when we turn from the kennel or the pigsty and watch the dainty way in which a cat takes its meals. That a cat allows people to approach it while it is feeding without showing jealousy proves that it does not attribute to human beings like tastes with its own.

The Alma (Kansas) Signal
Saturday, December 10, 1898, p4

The Origin of the Cat

It is impossible to trace the origin of the domestic cat with certainty to any existing species or variety of the wildcat. Indeed, the time at which the cat was first domesticated and introduced to human society is purely a matter of conjecture. Professor Shaler expresses the opinion that the domestication of the cat must have been much later than that of the dog, while other naturalists give reasons for believing to the contrary.

Some people agree with Professor Shaler, and for this reason: That dogs were probably first domesticated in order to assist in hunting, and, therefore, probably, in what is called the hunting age of human society, whereas the cat has nowhere been generally used as a hunting animal. The dog is essentially gregarious; he loves to hunt in packs, and when introduced to a human family he regards the family as his pack and hunts accordingly, so that he is easily made serviceable by the human hunter. The cat, on the contrary, is unsocial; it lives alone, hunts alone and feeds alone, so that it could not be expected to be easily trained to hunt either with men or for them. In fact, the only member of the cat family that is known to have been trained to hurt is the cheetah, though an ancient Egyptian painting, which may be seen in the British Museum, represents a cat which is apparently assisting a hunter to catch birds.

There is another reason for thinking that the cat must have been adopted by man after the hunting age, namely, the cat's wonderful attachment to locality. Animals like the wolf, with which the dog is most closely allied, follow their prey over vast tracts of country, and seem to be entirely destitute of local attachment. The wildcat, on the contrary, settles down in a particular spot and waits for its prey to come. When removed from its accustomed habitat, it seems to lose its skill, and therefore would be useless to men in a hunting age, because in that age men seldom had fixed habitations, but roamed abroad wherever game was to be found. Of course, much of this is conjecture. Whether the cat or the dog was first adopted by men cannot now be certainly known, but the cat was well known as a domestic animal at an early period of human history.

Abilene (Kansas) Daily Chronicle
Friday, March 11, 1898, p3

Feline Fun

Montaigne says: "When I play with my cat, how do I know whether she does not make a pastime of me, just as I do of her? We entertain ourselves with mutual antics; and if I have my own times of beginning and refusing, she, too, has hers." The sportiveness of kittens is exuberant, and makes them the most delightful of pets. Lindsay's remark is superfluous, except that it has to be made for the formal completeness of his treatise, that dogs and cats take part in the fun and frolic—sometimes rough or boisterous enough—of their child playfellows. They give every evidence, in fact, that such fun and frolic are the most enjoyed features of that period of their lives. As the animal matures, it becomes more sedate, and even assumes a meditative air, but the taste for sport dues not die out till infirmity begins to wear upon it. A cat mentioned in the *Animal World* would allow itself to be rolled up or swung about in a tablecloth, and seemed to enjoy the fun; and Wood's dignified Pusset would let his friends do anything they pleased with him—lift him by any part of the body, toss him in the air from one to another, use him as a footstool, boa or pillow, make him jump over their hands or leap on their shoulders, or walk along their extended arms, with perfect complacency. At the same time, he was keenly sensitive to ridicule, and, if laughed at, would walk off with every manifestation of offended dignity.

Lindsay names the cat as one of the animals that perpetrate practical jokes on each other or on man; that enter thoroughly into the spirit of the joke or fun, and enjoy and exult in its success; and cites in illustration of his principle an instance of a cat teasing a frog, seemingly to hear it cry. Tad, of Burnham, Maine, seems to have had the humorous sense in a more refined degree. He would sit in the yard, and, calling the neighboring cats together, would maneuver as though giving them orders, till he got them to fighting; then would withdraw to one side, or to his seat upon the window sill, and look on in evident amusement, swinging his large bushy tail forcibly against the window pane; but, when called into the house by his mistress, he always obeyed. — W.H. Larrabee in *Popular Science Monthly*

Deseret Evening News, Salt Lake City, Utah
Saturday, December 27, 1890, p4

About Cats

I hope you will never think lightly of a cat. A cat is about the only animal that will not endure to be deprived of its liberty. A cat would rather live in a barn, get its own living and have its freedom, than to be cooped up in the richest house and fed with the richest food. A cat wounded by a stick or stone, or caught in some trap from which it has either gnawed or pulled its way, and perhaps lost a paw, will crawl to some quiet, out-of-the-way place and endure in silence agony which no human being would endure and get well without a doctor. Some people starve cats to make them catch mice and rats. This is a great mistake, as they hunt for pleasure as much as for food, and if driven to hunger will not hunt but steal if they are kept about a house. If cats are well fed, and given meat once or twice a week, there will be very few rats or mice the on the premises.

Daily Capital Journal, Salem, Oregon
Wednesday, May13, 1896, p2

Chapter Nine

Catcalls

For the curtain call on *Cat Tales of the Old West*, humor seemed to be the best conclusion for these feline stories. Despite their nocturnal noise and many faults in the eyes of many pioneers, cats remained a source of pleasure and humor.

With pioneer life often hard and unrelenting, humor provided an outlet from the grind of day-to-day efforts to make ends meet or just survive. Some of the cat humor is grounded in the temperament of the cat and some in the character of the pioneer.

Humor at its core is a con job on the intellect or the common expectation. The following examples illustrate that trait, though the humor doesn't always transfer to contemporary times due to changing sensibilities and life experiences. Sometimes the frontier humor can bring a grin and on occasion a shrug or grimace.

Just as the first example in this collection of frontier perspectives on cats began with a poem by named author Bret Harte, the final chapter ends with another named author, though not as well-known as Harte. *The Poet to his Cat* by Rev. W.N. Clarke illustrates not only the talents employed to describe the feline breed, but the devotion of people to their cats. It seemed an appropriate choice to end this collection.

About Cats

"You are accused," said the Austin Recorder to the culprit, "of having fired a gun twice within the city limits. Did you kill or cripple anybody?"

"No, sir."

"It is a very serious matter to fire off a gun in the city limits and not kill anybody. Don't you know you are liable to be punished very severely for such carelessness?"

"Yes, your Honor; but there are some very mitigating circumstances."

"What are they, and how many of them are there?"

"They are cats, your Honor, and from the noise they make I should think there were about a thousand of them. They made a worse racket than Wash Jones and Ireland did when they had that joint gubernatorial discussion at Houston."

"So, you are troubled by cats?"

"Yes, your Honor, they worry me nearly to death, and I fired at them twice. That's how I came to violate the city ordinance."

Recorder (brightening up) — "Come here, prisoner, I wish to consult with you confidentially. Tell me, how many did you kill?"

"Three with the first barrel and two with the second."

"Splendid! Glorious! What size shot do you use when you violate the city ordinance by discharging firearms within the city limits?"

"I use duck shot; it fetches them every time."

"I'm glad to hear that. I've been using a size smaller when I violated the city ordinance. Would you object to lending me your gun?"

"I will lend it to you with pleasure," replied the prisoner, "but your Honor must remember that you are liable to be severely punished if you shoot off a gun inside the city and do not kill anybody."

"You can go, but do not let it happen again." — *Texas Siftings*

The Record-Union, Sacramento, California
Thursday, January 18, 1883, p4

Feline Exhibition

A citizen of Topeka is a collector of cats and has the largest "mewseum" in the United States.

The Advocate, Lakin, Kansas
Thursday, November 21, 1895, p2

Expensive Kitty

Dr. Adams of Hood River, has a $75 cat—at least that is what the cat cost him one night, in broken bottles and jars in his drug store.

The Vancouver (Washington) Independent
Thursday, February 7, 1878, p4

Scientific Ignorance

The ignorance of naturalists is … most conspicuously shown when they attempt to describe the cat. They learnedly inform us that the cat belongs to the species Felis *domestica*; that it is a carnivorous mammalian quadruped, capable of domestication, and with a passion for mice. This sounds well, but is very far from being an exhaustive description of the cat. Indeed, it is characterized by other errors than those of omission, and is in every way unsatisfactory.

The cat, above everything else, is a crockery-smashing animal. Its alleged passion for mice, which, by the way, is never manifested except when the cat is on the verge of starvation, is not to be named on the same day with its passion for breaking crockery, and the skill and perseverance which it shows in gratifying this passion are simply wonderful. — *Harper's Bazaar*
The Columbus (Nebraska) Journal
Wednesday, March 18, 1885, p1

Smile When You Say That

A Seymour, Indiana, man picked up a stick of cordwood the other night, and chased a cat across the back yard. He didn't catch the cat, but he caught the clothesline with his teeth, and now when he smiles the corners of his mouth pass each other at the back of his neck. — *Burlington Hawkeye*
Fort Scott (Kansas) Daily Monitor
Thursday, December 5, 1878, p2

Change of Heart

A Rugg street youngster who has been the possessor
of cats of several colors and sizes felt like having a
change, and so remarked to his mother the other day,
as he stroked the cat he held in his lap: "Mamma, I
hope the next cat I have will be a dog!" — *Messenger*
> *Great Falls (Montana) Weekly Tribune*
> Wednesday, June 8, 1887, p1

Cat and Mouse

A hungry Cat—
A foolish Rat.
A lively Run—
Exciting Fun.

Ferocious Jaws—
Remorseless Claws.
A dying Squeal—
A hearty Meal.

Alas, poor Rat!
O happy Cat!
> *Paradise (Texas) Messenger*
> Friday, December 30, 1881, p8

Chuckling Cats

The funniest thing in the career of the carousing cat is
when he sits on a back fence placidly watching a
woman trying to come within several miles of him

with a job lot of bric-a-brac.
Paradise (Texas) Messenger
Saturday, February 15, 1890, p7

Proper English

O why shall we say for catched, caught,
As grammarians some say we ought?
Let us see
How things be
When this kind of teaching is taught

The egg isn't hatched, it is haught;
My breeches aren't patched, they are paught;
John and Jane are not matched, they are maught;
My door isn't latched, it is laught;
The pie wasn't snatched, it was snaught;
The cat never scratched, but she scraught;
The roof wasn't thatched, it was thaught.

If English must this way be wrought,
It soon will be natched—that is nought.
The Record-Union, Sacramento, California
Monday, May 1, 1882, p4

Brevities

'Cause a cat is a cat;
  Can't she have any fun,
Without us yelling "Scat!"?
  'Cause a cat is a cat,
Must a boot-jack go spat;

Ere her fun has begun?
'Cause a cat is a cat,
  Can't she have any fun?
    The Daily Chronicle, Centralia, Washington
    Tuesday, July 10, 1894, p3

Not His Fault

Mamma: Johnnie, did you throw that cat in the well!
Johnnie: Indeed I didn't. I was just holdin' it over
the box by the tail and it wiggled loose and fell in. —
Washington Critic
    Paradise (Texas) Messenger
    Saturday, October 18, 1890, p6

Aroma of the Press

An exchange thinks there is nothing that smells much
worse than a dead cat. Did that editor ever smell the
editorial page of the *Atchison Champion*? Otherwise, he
should reserve his opinion until he has had a whiff of
that odor. It smells like two dead cats in an
uncleaned room of a Junction City hotel.
    Junction City (Kansas) Union
    Monday, August 1, 1887, p2

The Dog Tax

Editor Statesman: Is the demand for the revival of the dog tax wise? It was a vexatious tax, difficult of enforcement and for that reason, and the reason that the marshal didn't want to be a dog killer (who would?) was suffered to lapse into "innocuous desuetude." The amount of the tax received from that source would be very small, and would not compensate for the irritation it would cause. And why should dogs be taxed more than cats? Is it because they are more on the sidewalks? If so, they are not as much so as the bicycles, not so great a nuisance as these, and not so dangerous. Yet they invade the sidewalks and shins, and pay no tax or license. — *The Dogs*

Statesman Journal, Salem, Oregon
May 14, 1892, p2

Too Inquisitive

"What was cats made for, mother?" asked a little boy who had been scratched by a household tabby.

"Cats made for? Well, I suppose to kill mice."

"Who made "em?"

"God made them."

"What was mice made for?"

"What was mice made for? For some purpose, I suppose. For cats to catch, perhaps."

"Did God make the mice, too?"

"He did. He made all things."

"Well, if cats is made for catchin' mice, God wouldn't need to make cats if he hadn't made any mice, would he?"

"No, I suppose not."

"What made him make 'em for, then?"

"Make what?"

"The mice."

"Child, it's time for you to go to school. Hurry, or you'll be late."

The Morning Astorian, Astoria, Oregon
Wednesday, September 3, 1884, p3

The Cat Ate It

The story is told of a colored preacher who wanted to deliver a startling sermon. He had heard of sensational methods and determined to give his congregation a surprise. A small boy was taken into his confidence as a confederate and stationed on the roof just above the pulpit. In the lad's keep was entrusted a pigeon, which was to be let loose in the church from a convenient hole at the proper moment.

The church was packed and the preacher having stormed denouncement, raised his voice and cried: "And the Holy Ghost descended in the form of a dove," but no dove appeared. He repeated the sentence. Still no dove. At the third outcry a black face appeared at the hole in the roof and the query came: "Pa'son, a cat's done eat de holy ghost. But Is'e got de cat. Shall I throw'm down?"

The Weekly Chieftain, Vinita, Oklahoma
Thursday, July 13, 1899, p1

Tragic Chase

The cat in Camp County that has two heads and one body and tail, got after two mice the other day, and was incontinently killed and exploded when the two rodent took different routes for different holes a yard apart. Of course, the two halves of the feline were laid out just a yard apart, and the old woman that owned this cat says that the next of the sort, to avoid calamities of this painful nature, must be cross-eyed to keep the heads level.

> *The Austin (Texas) Weekly Statesman*
> Thursday, October 19, 1876, p2

They Don't Speak Now

They were engaged to be married and called each other by their first names. Tom and Fanny, and he was telling her how he had always liked the name of Fanny and how it sounded like music to his ears.

"I like the name so well," he added as a sort of clincher to the argument, "that when sister Clara asked him to name her pet terrier, I at once called it Fanny, after you, dearest."

"I don't think was very nice," said the fair girl, edging away from him. "How would you like to have a dog named alter you?"

"Why that's nothing," said Tom, airily, "half the cats in the country are named me."

> *Nevada State Journal*, Reno, Nevada
> Thursday, September 7, 1882, p2

Kitty vs. Hubby

During the excitement among the passengers at the railroad accident at Tremont, near Davisville, yesterday, a lady rushed around frantically, calling, "John! John! Oh, where's my husband?"

Immediately following her was a very-much excited ancient maiden lady, crying, "Kitty! kitty! Oh, where's my cat?" Evidently two very useful articles were lost.

The Record-Union, Sacramento, California
Thursday, November 15, 1883, p3

Sober Cat

"Talking about mean men," said Uncle David, "there's an old chum of mine whose boss gave him twenty-five cents to buy something for the store cat. He buys beer, and then says the cat won't touch it, and he has to drink it himself."

The Weekly Chieftain, Vinita, Oklahoma
Friday, September 29, 1882, p1

Hair-raising Experience

A cat farm has been established in Cincinnati. Its purr-puss is to raise fur.

Columbus (Nebraska) Journal
Wednesday, December 11, 1895, p4

Rays of Mirth

It is no indication that a cat knows the value of money, simply because it always carries its purrs with it.

Austin (Texas) Weekly Statesman
Thursday, April 9, 1885, p4

A Category of Felines

Fort Worth is fond of cats. She has the Gulf, Colorado & Santa Feline, the Atchison, Topeka & Santa Feline and would doubtless make a hard scratch for any other Feline that would stick its head across the state line. — *Dallas Tarantula*

Fort Worth (Texas) Daily Gazette
Wednesday, May 19, 1886, p2

Community Benevolence

Somebody at Claremore offers a reward of ten dollars for the return of a lost cat. Let us send over a thousand or two—it may be in the lot.

Muskogee (Oklahoma) Phoenix
Thursday, September 14, 1899, p3

Canine-Feline Relations

The Dog and the Cat are fighting. Is this wrong?

Yes, it is very wrong for the Dog and the Cat to fight because they are not married.

When you grow up, children, you will see the point of this lesson.

Arizona Weekly Citizen, Tucson, Arizona
Sunday, January 1, 1882, p1

No Secret

"How do you keep your cat
So sleek and fat?"
"Why, that's the least of labors.
We only have to keep
Him here to sleep,
He boards 'round with the neighbors." — *Chicago Tribune*

The Alma (Kansas) Enterprise
Friday, December 10, 1897, p6

The Poet to His Cat

Tuck in thy toes, prick up thine ears,
  Assume a listening attitude,
And I will tell thee, happy cat,
  The tale of thy beatitude,
And when I've told thee all the truth
  Just rub my hand in gratitude.

What hast thou to be thankful for
  Besides thy far famed fatitude"
Thou roamest free, with ample room,
  Not housed in crampling flatitude,
And thou has beds luxurious
  On couch and chair and matitude—
Beds which but for they hairs would be
  Adorned with neatest nattitude.
Thy days are passed in quietness,
  Unteased by brawling bratitude,
Nor even are thy nerves outworn
  By steady stream of chatitude.
Simple thy clothing, happy cat,
  Unvexed by styles in hatitude.
Well mayest thou pity other cats,
  Harried and worn by scatitude,
For friendly hands are stroking thee
  With touch of gentle patitude,
And never once has cruelty
  Stirred thee to pitapatitude.
Noble cat pleasures fill thy life
  And swell to high ecstatitude.
Thou meetest oft thy cattish kind
  And join'st in feline spatitude,
And when the felines go for thee
  Thou giv'st them titfortatitude,
And in the house thou mak'est thy boast
  Of cellars cleared of ratitude.
Let other cats their homes desert
  In folly blind as batitude.
Thou'lt never seek divorce from thine
  On grounds of incompatitude.

Now, cat, I've told thee all thy lot
  Of happy this and thatitude,
And I expect to see in thee
  Appreciative catitude. — Rev. W.N. Clarke in *St. Nicholas*

> *Western Liberal*, Lordsburg, New Mexico
> Friday, July 24, 1896, p4

ABOUT THE AUTHOR

Preston Lewis is the award-winning author of more than 50 nonfiction and fiction works, including westerns, historical novels and young adult novels. In 2021 he was inducted into the Texas Institute of Letters for his literary accomplishments.

Western Writers of America (WWA) has honored Lewis with two Spur Awards, one for best article and the second for best western. He has received nine Will Rogers Medallion Awards for traditional westerns, nonfiction articles, western humor and short stories.

Lewis is a past president of WWA and the West Texas Historical Association. He holds a bachelor's degree from Baylor University and a master's degree from Ohio State University, both in journalism. Additionally, he has a second master's degree in history from Angelo State University.

He lives in San Angelo, Texas, with wife Harriet.

E-mail: prestonlewisauthor@gmail.com
Facebook: prestonlewisauthor
Website: prestonlewisauthor.com